The

Series

John R. W. Stott (NT)

The Message of Galatians

Only One Way

Titles in this series

OLD TESTAMENT

The Message of **Genesis 1—11**
David Atkinson

The Message of **Genesis 12—50**
Joyce G. Baldwin

The Message of **Deuteronomy**
Raymond Brown

The Message of **Judges**
Michael Wilcock

The Message of **Ruth**
David Atkinson

The Message of **Chronicles**
Michael Wilcock

The Message of **Job**
David Atkinson

The Message of **Ecclesiastes**
Derek Kidner

The Message of **Jeremiah**
Derek Kidner

The Message of **Daniel**
Ronald S. Wallace

The Message of **Hosea**
Derek Kidner

The Message of **Amos**
J. A. Motyer

NEW TESTAMENT

The Message of the **Sermon on the Mount (Matthew 5—7)**
John R. W. Stott

The Message of **Mark**
Donald English

The Message of **Luke**
Michael Wilcock

The Message of **John**
Bruce Milne

The Message of **Acts**
John R. W. Stott

The Message of **1 Corinthians**
David Prior

The Message of **2 Corinthians**
Paul Barnett

The Message of **Galatians**
John R. W. Stott

The Message of **Ephesians**
John R. W. Stott

The Message of **Philippians**
J. A. Motyer

The Message of **Colossians & Philemon**
R. C. Lucas

The Message of **1 & 2 Thessalonians**
John R. W. Stott

The Message of **2 Timothy**
John R. W. Stott

The Message of **Hebrews**
Raymond Brown

The Message of **James**
J. A. Motyer

The Message of **1 Peter**
Edmund P. Clowney

The Message of **John's Letters**
David Jackman

The Message of **Revelation**
Michael Wilcock

The Message of Galatians

Only One Way

John R. W. Stott

Rector Emeritus of All Souls' Church, Langham Place, and Director of the London Institute for Contemporary Christianity

Inter-Varsity Press
Leicester, England
Downers Grove, Illinois, U.S.A.

Inter-Varsity Press
38 De Montfort Street, Leicester LE1 7GP, England
P.O. Box 1400, Downers Grove, Illinois 60515, U.S.A.

Inter-Varsity Press, England, is the publishing division of the Universities and Colleges Christian Fellowship (formerly the Inter-Varsity Fellowship), a student movement linking Christian Unions in universities and colleges throughout the United Kingdom and the Republic of Ireland, and a member movement of the International Fellowship of Evangelical Students. For information about local and national activities write to UCCF, 38 De Montfort Street, Leicester LE1 7GP.

InterVarsity Press, U.S.A., is the book-publishing division of Inter-Varsity Christian Fellowship, a student movement active on campus at hundreds of universities, colleges and schools of nursing. For information about local and regional activities, write IVCF, 233 Langdon St., Madison, WI 53703.

Cover photograph: Robert Cushman Hayes

Text set in Great Britain

UK ISBN 0-85110-734-6 (paperback)
USA ISBN 0-87784-288-4 (paperback)
USA ISBN 0-87784-925-0 (set of The Bible Speaks Today, paperback)

Library of Congress Cataloging in Publication Data

Stott, John R. W.
The message of Galatians.

(The Bible speaks today)
Originally published under title: Only one way.
Bibliography: p.
1. Bible. N.T. Galatians—Commentaries. I. Title.
BL2685.3.S86 1986 227'.4077 86-15173
ISBN 0-87784-288-4 (U.S.: pbk.)

---

26 25 24 23 22 21 20 19 18 17 16 15 14 13 12

14 13 12 11 10 09 08 07 06 05 04 03 02 01

CONTENTS

ACKNOWLEDGMENT

The Bible text in this publication is from the Revised Standard Version of the Bible, copyrighted in 1946 and 1952 by the Division of Christian Education, National Council of the Churches of Christ in the USA, and used by permission.

General preface

The Bible Speaks Today describes a series of both Old Testament and New Testament expositions, which are characterized by a threefold ideal: to expound the biblical text with accuracy, to relate it to contemporary life, and to be readable.

These books are, therefore, not 'commentaries', for the commentary seeks rather to elucidate the text than to apply it, and tends to be a work rather of reference than of literature. Nor, on the other hand, do they contain the kind of 'sermons' which attempt to be contemporary and readable, without taking Scripture seriously enough.

The contributors to this series are all united in their convictions that God still speaks through what he has spoken, and that nothing is more necessary for the life, health and growth of Christians than that they should hear what the Spirit is saying to them through his ancient—yet ever modern—Word.

J. A. MOTYER
J. R. W. STOTT
Series Editors

CHIEF ABBREVIATIONS

Arndt-Gingrich	*A Greek-English Lexicon of the New Testament and Other Early Christian Literature* translated and edited by W. F. Arndt and F. W. Gingrich (Cambridge University Press, 1957).
AV	English Authorized Version (King James), 1611.
Brown	*An Exposition of the Epistle to the Galatians* by John Brown, 1853 (The Sovereign Grace Book Club, 1957).
Cole	*The Epistle of Paul to the Galatians* by R. Alan Cole (*Tyndale New Testament Commentaries*, Tyndale Press, 1965).
Grimm-Thayer	*A Greek–English Lexicon of the New Testament* by C. L. W. Grimm and J. H. Thayer (Clark, 1901).
Hunter	*Galatians to Colossians* by A. M. Hunter (*Layman's Bible Commentaries*, S.C.M. Press, 1960).
JBP	*The New Testament in Modern English* by J. B. Phillips, 1947–58.
Liddell and Scott	*Greek–English Lexicon* compiled by H. G. Liddell and R. Scott. New Edition by H. S. Jones (Oxford University Press, 1925–40).
Lightfoot	*Saint Paul's Epistle to the Galatians* by J. B. Lightfoot, 1865 (Oliphants, 1957).
Luther	*Commentary on the Epistle to the Galatians* by Martin Luther, based on lectures delivered by him in 1531 (James Clarke, 1953).
LXX	Septuagint (pre-Christian Greek version of the Old Testament).
Moulton and Milligan	*The Vocabulary of the Greek New Testament* by J. H. Moulton and G. Milligan (Hodder and Stoughton, 1930).

NEB	New English Bible: New Testament, 1961.
Neill	*Paul to the Galatians* by Stephen C. Neill (*World Christian Books*, Lutterworth, 1958).
RSV	American Revised Standard Version, 1946–52.

1:1–5

THE APOSTLE PAUL'S AUTHORITY AND GOSPEL

PAUL an apostle—not from men nor through man, but through Jesus Christ and God the Father, who raised him from the dead—[2] *and all the brethren who are with me,*

To the churches of Galatia:

[3] *Grace to you and peace from God the Father and our Lord Jesus Christ,* [4] *who gave himself for our sins to deliver us from the present evil age, according to the will of our God and Father;* [5] *to whom be the glory for ever and ever. Amen.*

IN the course of the thirty years or so which elapsed between his conversion outside Damascus and his imprisonment in Rome, the apostle Paul travelled widely through the Empire as an ambassador of Jesus Christ. On his three famous missionary journeys he preached the gospel and planted churches in the provinces of Galatia, Asia, Macedonia (Northern Greece) and Achaia (Southern Greece). Moreover, his visits were followed by his letters, by which he helped to supervise the churches he had founded.

One of these letters, which many believe to be the earliest that he wrote (about AD 48 or 49), is the Epistle to the Galatians. It is addressed *To the churches of Galatia* (verse 2). There is some dispute among scholars as to what is meant by 'Galatia', and for the details here I must refer you to the commentaries. I myself take the view that the reference is to the southern part of the province, and in particular to the four cities of Pisidian Antioch, Iconium, Lystra and Derbe, which Paul evangelized during his first missionary journey. You can read about this in Acts 13 and 14.

In each city there was now a church. It is recognized in the New Testament that what is called 'the church of God' (Gal. 1:13), the universal church, is divided into local 'churches'. Not, of course, into denominations, but into congregations. The New English

Bible translates the phrase in verse 2 'to the Christian congregations of Galatia'. Further, these churches were grouped together because of geographical and political considerations. Such a group of churches could be described either in the plural (*e.g.* 'the churches of Galatia', 'the churches . . . in Judea', Gal. 1:2 and 22) or by a singular collective noun (*e.g.* 'Achaia', 2 Cor. 9:2). This usage seems to supply some biblical warrant for the concept of a regional church, the federation of local churches in a particular area.

Already in the first paragraph of his letter to the Galatians Paul touches on two themes to which he will constantly return, his apostleship and his gospel. In the ancient world all letters began with the writer's name, followed by the recipient's name and a greeting or message. But Paul enlarges in the Galatian Epistle more than was customary in those days, and more than he does in his other Epistles, both on his credentials as a writer and on his message. He has good reasons for doing so.

Since his visit to these Galatian cities the churches which he had founded had been troubled by false teachers. These men had mounted a powerful attack on Paul's authority and gospel. They contradicted his gospel of justification by grace alone through faith alone, insisting that for salvation more than faith in Christ was needed. You had to be circumcised as well, they said, and keep all the law of Moses (see Acts 15:1, 5). Having undermined Paul's gospel, they proceeded to undermine his authority also. 'Who is this fellow Paul, anyway?' they asked scornfully. 'He certainly wasn't one of the twelve apostles of Jesus. Nor, so far as we know, has he received any authorization from anybody. He is just a self-appointed impostor.'

Paul sees clearly the dangers of this two-pronged attack, and so he plunges, right at the beginning of the Epistle, into a statement of his apostolic authority and of his gospel of grace. He will elaborate these themes later in the Epistle, but notice how he begins: *Paul an apostle* (not an impostor) . . . *grace to you.* These two terms 'apostle' and 'grace' were loaded words in that situation, and if we understand their meaning, we have grasped the two main subjects of the Galatian Epistle.

1. PAUL'S AUTHORITY (verses 1, 2)

Paul an apostle—not from men nor through man, but through Jesus Christ and God the Father, who raised him from the dead—and all the brethren who are with me, To the churches of Galatia. Paul claims for himself the very title which the false teachers were evidently denying him. He was an apostle, an apostle of Jesus Christ. The term already had a precise connotation. 'To the Jew the word was well defined; it meant a special messenger, with a special status, enjoying an authority and commission that came from a body higher than himself.'[1]

This is the title which Jesus used for His special representatives or delegates. From the wider company of disciples He chose twelve, named them 'apostles', and sent them out to preach (Lk. 6:13; Mk. 3:14). Thus they were personally chosen, called and commissioned by Jesus Christ, and authorized to teach in His name. The New Testament evidence is clear that this group was small and unique. The word 'apostle' was not a general word which could be applied to every Christian like the words 'believer', 'saint' or 'brother'. It was a special term reserved for the Twelve and for one or two others whom the risen Christ had personally appointed. There can, therefore, be no apostolic succession, other than a loyalty to the apostolic doctrine of the New Testament. The apostles had no successors. In the nature of the case no-one could succeed them. They were unique.

To this select company of apostles Paul claimed to belong. We should get used to calling him 'the apostle Paul' rather than 'Saint Paul', because every Christian is a saint in New Testament vocabulary, while no Christian today is an apostle. Notice how he clearly distinguishes himself from other Christians who were with him at the time of writing. He calls them, in verse 2, *all the brethren who are with me.* He is happy to associate them with him in the salutation, but he unashamedly puts himself first and gives himself a title which he does not give to them. They are all 'brethren'; he alone among them is 'an apostle'.

He leaves us in no doubt about the nature of his apostleship. In other Epistles he is content to describe himself as 'called to be an

[1] Cole, p. 31.

apostle' (Rom. 1:1) or 'called by the will of God to be an apostle of Christ Jesus' (1 Cor. 1:1). Or, without mentioning his call, he styles himself 'an apostle of Jesus Christ by the will (or 'command') of God' (*cf.* 2 Cor. 1:1; Eph. 1:1; Col. 1:1; 1 Tim. 1:1; 2 Tim. 1:1). Here, however, at the beginning of the Galatian Epistle, he enlarges on his description of himself. He makes a forceful statement that his apostleship is not human in any sense, but essentially divine. Literally, he says that he is an apostle 'not from men nor through a man'. That is, he was not appointed by a group of men, such as the Twelve or the church at Jerusalem or the church at Antioch, as, for instance, the Jewish Sanhedrin appointed apostles, official delegates commissioned to travel and teach in their name. Paul himself (as Saul of Tarsus) had been one of these, as is plain from Acts 9:1, 2. But he had not been appointed to Christian apostleship by any group of men. Nor even, granted the divine origin of his apostolic appointment, was it brought to him through any individual human mediator, such as Ananias or Barnabas or anybody else. Paul insists that human beings had nothing whatever to do with it. His apostolic commission was human neither directly nor indirectly; it was wholly divine.

It was, in his words, *through Jesus Christ and God the Father, who raised him from the dead.* Only one preposition is used: '*through* Jesus Christ and God the Father.' But the contrast with the phrase 'from men' and 'through man' suggests that Paul's apostolic appointment came not from men but from God the Father, nor through a man, but through Jesus Christ (the inference being, incidentally, that Jesus Christ is not just a man). We know from elsewhere that this was the case. God the Father chose Paul to be an apostle (his call was 'by the will of God') and appointed him to this office through Jesus Christ, whom He raised from the dead. It was the risen Lord who commissioned him on the Damascus road, and Paul several times refers to this sight of the risen Christ as an essential condition of his apostleship (see 1 Cor. 9:1; 15:8, 9).

Why did Paul thus assert and defend his apostleship? Was he just a braggart, inflated with personal vanity? No. Was it from pique that men had dared to challenge his authority? No. It was because the gospel that he preached was at stake. If Paul were not an apostle of Jesus Christ, then men could, and no doubt would, reject his gospel. This he could not bear. For what Paul spoke was Christ's message on Christ's authority. So he defended his apostolic authority in order to defend his message.

This special, divine authority of the apostle Paul is enough in itself to discredit and dispose of certain modern views of the New Testament. Let me mention two.

a. The radical view

The view of modern radical theologians can be simply stated like this: The apostles were merely first-century witnesses to Jesus Christ. We on the other hand are twentieth-century witnesses, and our witness is just as good as theirs, if not better. So they read passages in the Epistles of Paul which they do not like, and they say: 'Well, that is Paul's view. My view is different.' They speak as if they were apostles of Jesus Christ and as if they had equal authority with the apostle Paul to teach and to decide what is true and right. Let me give you an example from a contemporary radical: 'St. Paul and St. John', he writes, 'were men of like passions to ourselves. However great their inspiration, . . . being human, their inspiration was not even or uniform. . . . For with their inspiration went that degree of psycho-pathology which is the common lot of all men. They too had their inner axes to grind of which they were unaware. What therefore they tell us must have a self-authenticating quality, like music. If it doesn't, we must be prepared to refuse it. We must have the courage to disagree.'[1] We are told to disagree, you observe, on purely subjective grounds. We are to prefer our own taste to the authority of Christ's apostles.

Again, Professor C. H. Dodd, who has made a great contribution to the biblical theology movement, nevertheless writes in the Introduction to his commentary on the Epistle to the Romans: 'Sometimes I think Paul is wrong, and I have ventured to say so.'[2] But we have no liberty to think or venture thus. The apostles of Jesus Christ were unique—unique in their experience of the Jesus of history, unique in their sight of the risen Lord, unique in their commission by Christ's authority and unique in their inspiration by

[1] From the chapter entitled 'Psychological Objections', by H. A. Williams, in *Objections to Christian Belief* (Constable, 1963), pp. 55, 56.

[2] *The Epistle to the Romans*, by C. H. Dodd (*Moffatt New Testament Commentary*, Hodder, 1932), pp. xxxiv, xxxv.

Christ's Spirit. We may not exalt our opinions over theirs or claim that our authority is as great as theirs. For their opinions and authority are Christ's. If we would bow to His authority, we must therefore bow to theirs. As He Himself said, 'he who receives you receives me' (Mt. 10:40; Jn. 13:20).

b. The Roman Catholic view

The Roman Catholics teach that, since the Bible authors were churchmen, the church wrote the Bible. Therefore the church is over the Bible and has authority not only to interpret it, but also to supplement it. But it is misleading to say that the church wrote the Bible. The apostles, the authors of the New Testament, were apostles of Christ, not of the church, and they wrote their letters as apostles of Christ, not of the church. Paul did not begin this Epistle 'Paul an apostle of the church, commissioned by the church to write to you Galatians'. On the contrary, he is careful to maintain that his commission and his message were from God; they were not from any man or group of men, such as the church. See also verses 11 and 12.

So the biblical view is that the apostles derived their authority from God through Christ. Apostolic authority is divine authority. It is neither human, nor ecclesiastical. And because it is divine, we must submit to it.

We turn now from Paul's credentials as a writer to his purpose in writing, from his authority to his gospel.

2. PAUL'S GOSPEL (verses 3, 4)

Grace to you and peace from God the Father and our Lord Jesus Christ. . . . Paul sends the Galatians a message of grace and peace, as in all his Epistles. But these are no formal and meaningless terms. Although 'grace' and 'peace' are common monosyllables, they are pregnant with theological substance. In fact, they summarize Paul's gospel of salvation. The nature of salvation is peace, or reconciliation—peace with God, peace with men, peace within. The source of salvation is grace, God's free favour, irrespective of any human merit or works, His loving-kindness to the undeserving. And this grace and peace flow from the Father and the Son together.

Paul immediately goes on to the great historical event in which

God's grace was exhibited and from which His peace is derived, namely the death of Jesus Christ on the cross. Verse 4: *who gave himself for our sins to deliver us from the present evil age, according to the will of our God and Father.* Although Paul has declared that God the Father raised Christ from the dead (verse 1), he writes now that it was by giving Himself to die on the cross that He saves us. Let us consider the rich teaching which is given here about the death of Christ.

a. Christ died for our sins

The character of His death is indicated in the expression *who gave himself for our sins.* The New English Bible translates 'who sacrificed himself for our sins'. The death of Jesus Christ was primarily neither a display of love, nor an example of heroism, but a sacrifice for sin. Indeed, the use in some of the best manuscripts of the preposition *peri* in the phrase 'for our sins' may be an echo of the Old Testament expression for the sin-offering.[1] The New Testament teaches that Christ's death was a sin-offering, the unique sacrifice by which our sins may be forgiven and put away. This great truth is not explained here, but later in the Epistle (3:13) we are told that Christ actually became 'a curse for us'. He bore in His righteous person the curse or judgment which our sins deserved.

Martin Luther comments that 'these words are very thunderclaps from heaven against all kinds of righteousness',[2] that is, all forms of self-righteousness. Once we have seen that Christ 'gave himself for our sins', we realize that we are sinners unable to save ourselves, and we give up trusting in ourselves that we are righteous.

b. Christ died to rescue us from this present age

If the nature of Christ's death on the cross was 'for our sins', its object was 'to rescue us out of this present age of wickedness' (verse 4, NEB). Bishop J. B. Lightfoot writes that the verb ('deliver', 'rescue') 'strikes the keynote of the epistle'. 'The Gospel is a rescue,' he adds, 'an emancipation from a state of bondage.'[3]

[1] LXX *peri hamartias, e.g.* Lv. 5:11 and Nu. 8:8. *Cf.* Rom. 8:3 and 1 Pet. 3:18, where the preposition is again *peri.*
[2] Luther, p. 47. [3] Lightfoot, p. 73.

Christianity is, in fact, a rescue religion. The Greek verb in this verse is a strong one (*exaireō*, in the middle voice). It is used in the Acts of the rescue of the Israelites from their Egyptian slavery (7:34), of the rescue of Peter both from prison and from the hand of Herod the King (12:11), and of the rescue of Paul from an infuriated mob about to lynch him (23:27). This verse in Galatians is the only place where it is used metaphorically of salvation. Christ died to rescue us.

From what does He rescue us by His death? Not out of 'this present evil *world*', as the Authorized Version puts it. For God's purpose is not to take us out of the world, but that we should stay in it and be both 'the light of the world' and 'the salt of the earth'. But Christ died to rescue us 'out of this present *age* of wickedness' (NEB), or, as perhaps it should be rendered, 'out of this present age of the wicked one', since he (the devil) is its lord. Let me explain this. The Bible divides history into two ages: 'this age' and 'the age to come'. It tells us, moreover, that 'the age to come' has come already, because Christ inaugurated it, although the present age has not yet finally passed away. So the two ages are running their course in parallel. They overlap one another. Christian conversion means being rescued from the old age and being transferred into the new age, 'the age to come'. And the Christian life is living in this age the life of the age to come.

The purpose of Christ's death, therefore, was not only to bring us forgiveness, but that, having been forgiven, we should live a new life, the life of the age to come. Christ *gave himself for our sins to deliver us from the present evil age*.

c. Christ died according to God's will

Having considered the nature and object of Christ's death, we come to its source or origin. It happened *according to the will of our God and Father*. Both our rescue out of this present evil age and the means by which it has been effected are according to the will of God. They are certainly not according to *our* will, as if we had achieved our own rescue. Nor are they just according to *Christ's* will, as if the Father were reluctant to act. In the cross the will of the Father and the will of the Son were in perfect harmony. We must never imply either that the Son volunteered to do something against the Father's will, or that the Father required the Son to do something against His own will. Paul writes both that the Son 'sacrificed himself' (verse 4a) and that His self-sacrifice was 'according to the will of our God and Father' (verse 4b).

In summary, this verse teaches that the nature of Christ's death is a sacrifice for sin, its object our rescue out of this present evil age, and its origin the gracious will of the Father and the Son.

CONCLUSION

What the apostle has in fact done in these introductory verses of the Epistle is to trace three stages of divine action for man's salvation. Stage 1 is the death of Christ for our sins to rescue us out of this present evil age. Stage 2 is the appointment of Paul as an apostle to bear witness to the Christ who thus died and rose again. Stage 3 is the gift to us who believe of the grace and peace which Christ won and Paul witnessed to.

At each of these three stages the Father and the Son have acted or continue to act together. The sin-bearing death of Jesus was both an act of self-sacrifice and according to the will of God the Father. The apostolic authority of Paul was 'through Jesus Christ and God the Father who raised him from the dead'. And the grace and peace which we enjoy as a result are also 'from God the Father and our Lord Jesus Christ'. How beautiful this is! Here is our God, the living God, the Father and the Son, at work in grace for our salvation. First, He achieved it in history at the cross. Next, He has announced it in Scripture through His chosen apostles. Thirdly, He bestows it in experience upon believers today. Each stage is indispensable. There could be no Christian experience today without the unique work of Christ on the cross, uniquely witnessed to by the apostles. Christianity is both a historical and an experimental religion. Indeed, one of its chief glories is this marriage between history and experience, between the past and the present. We must never attempt to divorce them. We cannot do without the work of Christ, nor can we do without the witness of Christ's apostles, if we want to enjoy Christ's grace and peace today.

No wonder Paul ends his first paragraph with a doxology: *to whom be the glory* (the glory which is His due, the glory which belongs to Him) *for ever and ever. Amen.*

1:6–10

FALSE TEACHERS AND FAITHLESS GALATIANS

I AM astonished that you are so quickly deserting him who called you in the grace of Christ and turning to a different gospel—[7] *not that there is another gospel, but there are some who trouble you and want to pervert the gospel of Christ.* [8] *But even if we, or an angel from heaven, should preach to you a gospel contrary to that which we preached to you, let him be accursed.* [9] *As we have said before, so now I say again, If any one is preaching to you a gospel contrary to that which you received, let him be accursed.*

[10] *Am I now seeking the favour of men, or of God? Or am I trying to please men? If I were still pleasing men, I should not be a servant of Christ.*

AFTER greeting his readers, in every other Epistle Paul goes on to pray for them or to praise and thank God. Only in the Epistle to the Galatians are there no prayer, no praise, no thanksgiving and no commendation. Instead he addresses himself at once to his theme with a note of extreme urgency. He expresses astonishment at the fickleness and instability of the Galatians. He goes on to complain about the false teachers who were troubling the Galatian churches. And then he utters a most solemn, fearful anathema upon those who dare to change the gospel.

1. THE UNFAITHFULNESS OF THE GALATIANS (verse 6)

I am astonished that you are so quickly deserting him who called you in the grace of Christ. 'Ye are . . . removed' (AV) is misleading, because the verb should be active not passive (it is in the middle voice), and the tense should be present, not past. It means not 'you are so soon removed' but 'you are so quickly deserting' or, as the New English Bible puts it, you are 'turning so quickly away'. The Greek word (*metatithēmi*) is an interesting one. It signifies 'to transfer one's allegiance'. It is used of soldiers in the army who revolt or desert, and of men who change sides in politics or philosophy. Thus, a certain Dionysius of Heracleia, who left the Stoics to become a member of the rival philosophical school, an Epicurean, was called *ho metathemenos*, a 'turncoat'.[1]

It is of this that Paul accuses the Galatians. They are religious turncoats, spiritual deserters. They are turning away from Him who had called them in the grace of Christ and are embracing another gospel. The true gospel is in its essence what Paul called it in Acts 20:24, 'the gospel of the grace of God'. It is good news of a God who is gracious to undeserving sinners. In grace He gave His Son to die for us. In grace He calls us to Himself. In grace He justifies us when we believe. 'All is from God', as Paul wrote in 2 Corinthians 5:18, meaning that 'all is of grace'. Nothing is due to our efforts, merits or works; everything in salvation is due to the grace of God.

But the Galatian converts, who had received this gospel of grace, were now turning away to another gospel, a gospel of works. The false teachers were evidently 'Judaizers', whose 'gospel' is summarized in Acts 15:1: 'Unless you are circumcised according to the custom of Moses, you cannot be saved.' They did not deny that you must believe in Jesus for salvation, but they stressed that you must be circumcised and keep the law as well. In other words, you must let Moses finish what Christ has begun. Or rather, you yourself must finish, by your obedience to the law, what Christ has begun. You must add your works to the work of Christ. You must finish Christ's unfinished work.

This doctrine Paul simply will not tolerate. What? Add human merits to the merit of Christ and human works to the work of Christ? God forbid! The work of Christ is a finished work; and the gospel of Christ is a gospel of free grace. Salvation is by grace alone, through faith alone, without any admixture of human works or merits. It is due solely to God's gracious call, and not to any good works of our own.

Paul goes further than this. He says that the defection of the Galatian converts was in their experience as well as in their theology. He accuses them not of deserting the gospel of grace for another gospel, but of 'deserting *him* who called' them in grace. In other words, theology and experience, Christian faith and Christian life, belong together and cannot be separated. To turn from the gospel

[1] See *metatithēmi* in Moulton and Milligan.

of grace is to turn from the God of grace. Let the Galatians beware, who have so readily and rashly started turning away. It is impossible to forsake it (the gospel) without forsaking Him (God). As Paul says later, in Galatians 5:4, 'You have fallen away from grace.'

2. THE ACTIVITY OF THE FALSE TEACHERS (verse 7)

The reason why the Galatian converts were deserting God who had called them in grace was that *there are some who trouble you* (verse 7b). The Greek verb for 'trouble' (*tarassō*) means to 'shake' or 'agitate'. The Galatian congregations had been thrown by the false teachers into a state of turmoil—intellectual confusion on the one hand and warring factions on the other. It is rather interesting that the Council at Jerusalem, which probably met just after Paul had written this Epistle, were to use the same verb in their letter to the churches: 'We have heard that some persons from us have *troubled* you with words, unsettling your minds, although we gave them no instructions' (Acts 15:24).

This trouble was caused by false doctrine. The Judaizers were trying to 'pervert' (AV, RSV) or 'distort' (NEB) the gospel. They were propagating what J. B. Phillips calls 'a travesty of the gospel of Christ'. As a matter of fact, the Greek word (*metastrepsai*) is even stronger still. It could be translated 'to reverse'. In this case, they were not just corrupting the gospel, but actually 'reversing' it, turning it back to front and upside down. You cannot modify or supplement the gospel without radically changing its character.

So the two chief characteristics of the false teachers are that they were troubling the church and changing the gospel. These two go together. To tamper with the gospel is always to trouble the church. You cannot touch the gospel and leave the church untouched, because the church is created and lives by the gospel. Indeed, the church's greatest troublemakers (now as then) are not those outside who oppose, ridicule and persecute it, but those inside who try to change the gospel. It is they who trouble the church. Conversely, the only way to be a good churchman is to be a good gospel-man. The best way to serve the church is to believe and to preach the gospel.

3. THE REACTION OF THE APOSTLE PAUL (verses 8–10)

The situation in the Galatian churches should by now be clear. False teachers were distorting the gospel, so that Paul's converts were deserting it. The apostle's first reaction was one of utter astonishment. Verse 6: *I am astonished that you are so quickly deserting him who called you in the grace of Christ.* Many evangelists of later generations have been similarly astonished and distressed to see how quickly, how readily converts relax their hold of the gospel which they seemed to have so firmly embraced. It is, as Paul writes in Galatians 3:1, as if someone has bewitched them, cast a spell over them; and this is, in fact, the case. The devil disturbs the church as much by error as by evil. When he cannot entice Christian people into sin, he deceives them with false doctrine.

Paul's second reaction was indignation over the false teachers, upon whom he now pronounces a solemn curse. Verses 8 and 9: *But even if we, or an angel from heaven, should preach to you a gospel contrary to that which we preached to you, let him be accursed. As we have said before, so now I say again, If any one is preaching to you a gospel contrary to that which you received, let him be accursed.* The Greek word twice translated 'accursed' is *anathema.* It was used in the Greek Old Testament for the divine ban, the curse of God resting upon anything or anyone devoted by Him to destruction. The story of Achan provides an example of this. God said that the spoil of the Canaanites was under His ban—it was devoted to destruction. But Achan stole and kept for himself what should have been destroyed.

So the apostle Paul desires that these false teachers should come under the divine ban, curse or *anathema.* That is, he expresses the wish that God's judgment will fall upon them. The Galatian churches, it is implied, will surely then not accord such teachers a welcome or a hearing, but refuse to receive or listen to them, because they are men whom God has rejected (*cf.* 2 Jn. 10, 11).

What are we to say about this *anathema*? Are we to dismiss it as an intemperate outburst? Are we to reject it as a sentiment inconsistent with the Spirit of Christ and unworthy of the gospel of Christ? Are we to explain it away as the utterance of a man who was the child of his age and knew no better? Many people would, but at least two considerations indicate that this apostolic *anathema* was not the expression of personal venom towards rival teachers.

The first is that the curse of the apostle, or the curse of God which the apostle desires, is universal in its embrace. It rests upon any and every teacher who distorts the essence of the gospel and propagates his distortion. This is clear in verse 9, 'As we have said before, so now I say again, If *any one* is preaching. . . .' There is no exception. In verse 8 he specifically applies it to *angels* as well as men, and then adds himself also: 'But even if *we*. . . .' So disinterested is Paul's zeal for the gospel, that he even desires the curse of God to fall upon *himself*, should he be guilty of perverting it. The fact that he thus includes himself clears him of the charge of personal spite or animosity.

The second consideration is that his curse is uttered deliberately and with conscious responsibility to God. For one thing, it is expressed twice (verses 8 and 9). As John Brown, the nineteenth-century Scottish commentator, writes: 'The apostle repeats it to show the Galatians that this was no excessive, exaggerated statement, into which passion had hurried him, but his calmly formed and unalterable opinion.'[1] Then Paul goes on in verse 10: *Am I now seeking the favour of men, or of God? Or am I trying to please men? If I were still pleasing men, I should not be a servant of Christ.* It seems that his detractors had accused him of being a time-server, a man-pleaser, who suited his message to his audience. But is this outspoken condemnation of the false teachers the language of a man-pleaser? On the contrary, no man can serve two masters. And since Paul is first and foremost a servant of Jesus Christ, his ambition is to please Christ, not men. It is therefore as 'a servant of Christ', responsible to his divine Lord, that he measures his words and dares to utter this solemn *anathema*.

We have seen, then, that Paul uttered his *anathema* both impartially (whoever the teachers might be) and deliberately (in the presence of Christ his Lord).

Yet somebody may ask, 'Why did he feel so strongly and use such drastic language?' Two reasons are plain. The first is that the glory of Christ was at stake. To make men's works necessary to salvation, even as a supplement to the work of Christ, is derogatory to His finished work. It is to imply that Christ's work was in some way unsatisfactory, and that men need to add to it and improve on it. It is, in effect, to declare the cross redundant: 'if justification

[1] Brown, p. 48.

were through the law, then Christ died to no purpose' (Gal. 2:21).

The second reason why Paul felt this matter so keenly is that the good of men's souls was also at stake. He was not writing about some trivial doctrine, but about something that is fundamental to the gospel. Nor was he speaking of those who merely *hold* false views, but of those who *teach* them and mislead others by their teaching. Paul cared deeply for the souls of men. In Romans 9:3 he declared that he would be willing himself to be accursed (literally, to be *anathema*), if thereby others could be saved. He knew that the gospel of Christ is the power of God unto salvation. Therefore to corrupt the gospel was to destroy the way of salvation and so to send to ruin souls who might have been saved by it. Did not Jesus Himself utter a solemn warning to the person who causes others to stumble, saying that 'it would be better for him if a great millstone were hung round his neck and he were thrown into the sea' (Mk. 9:42)? It seems then that Paul, far from contradicting the Spirit of Christ, was actually expressing it. Of course we live in an age in which it is considered very narrow-minded and intolerant to have any clear and strong opinions of one's own, let alone to disagree sharply with anybody else. As for actually desiring false teachers to fall under the curse of God and be treated as such by the church, the very idea is to many inconceivable. But I venture to say that if we cared more for the glory of Christ and for the good of the souls of men, we too would not be able to bear the corruption of the gospel of grace.

CONCLUSION

The lesson which stands out from this paragraph is that there is only one gospel. The popular view is that there are many different ways to God, that the gospel changes with the changing years, and that you must not condemn the gospel to fossilization in the first century AD. But Paul would not endorse these notions. He insists here that there is only one gospel and that this gospel does not change. Any teaching that claims to be 'another gospel' is 'not another' (verses 6, 7, AV). In order to make this point, he uses the two adjectives *heteros* ('another' in the sense of 'different') and *allos* ('another' in the sense of 'a second'). The Revised Standard Version brings it out: 'You are turning to a different gospel—not that there is another gospel.' In other words, there are certainly different gospels being preached, but this is what they are—*different*. There is not another, a second; there is only one. The message of the false teachers was not an alternative gospel; it was a perverted gospel.

How can we recognize the true gospel? Its marks are given us here. They concern its substance (what it is) and its source (where it comes from).

a. The substance of the gospel

It is the gospel of grace, of God's free and unmerited favour. To turn from Him who called you in the grace of Christ is to turn from the true gospel. Whenever teachers start exalting man, implying that he can contribute anything to his salvation by his own morality, religion, philosophy or respectability, the gospel of grace is being corrupted. That is the first test. The true gospel magnifies the free grace of God.

b. The source of the gospel

The second test concerns the gospel's origin. The true gospel is the gospel of the apostles of Jesus Christ, in other words, the New Testament gospel. Look again at verses 8 and 9. Paul's *anathema* is pronounced on anybody who preaches a gospel which is either 'contrary to that which we preached to you' or 'contrary to that which you received'. That is to say, the norm, the criterion, by which all systems and opinions are to be tested, is the primitive gospel, the gospel which the apostles preached and which is now recorded in the New Testament. Any system 'other . . . than' (AV), or 'contrary to' (RSV), or 'at variance with' (NEB) this apostolic gospel is to be rejected.

This is the second fundamental test. Anybody who rejects the apostolic gospel, no matter who he may be, is himself to be rejected. He may appear as 'an angel from heaven'. In this case we are to prefer apostles to angels. We are not to be dazzled, as many people are, by the person, gifts or office of teachers in the church. They may come to us with great dignity, authority and scholarship. They may be bishops or archbishops, university professors or even the pope himself. But if they bring a gospel other than the gospel preached by the apostles and recorded in the New Testament, they are to be rejected. We judge them by the gospel; we do not judge the gospel by them. As Dr. Alan Cole expresses it, 'The outward person of the messenger does not validate his message; rather, the nature of the message validates the messenger.'[1]

So then, as we hear the multifarious views of men and women today, spoken, written, broadcast and televised, we must subject each of them to these two rigorous tests. Is their opinion consistent with the free grace of God and with the plain teaching of the New Testament? If not, we must reject it, however august the teacher may be. But if it passes these tests, then let us embrace it and hold it fast. We must not compromise it like the Judaizers, nor desert it like the Galatians, but live by it ourselves and seek to make it known to others.

[1] Cole, pp. 41, 59.

1:11–24

THE ORIGINS OF PAUL'S GOSPEL

FOR *I would have you know, brethren, that the gospel which was preached by me is not man's gospel.* [12] *For I did not receive it from man, nor was I taught it, but it came through a revelation of Jesus Christ.* [13] *For you have heard of my former life in Judaism, how I persecuted the church of God violently and tried to destroy it;* [14] *and I advanced in Judaism beyond many of my own age among my people, so extremely zealous was I for the traditions of my fathers.* [15] *But when he who had set me apart before I was born, and had called me through his grace,* [16] *was pleased to reveal his Son to me, in order that I might preach him among the Gentiles, I did not confer with flesh and blood,* [17] *nor did I go up to Jerusalem to those who were apostles before me, but I went away into Arabia; and again I returned to Damascus.*

[18] *Then after three years I went up to Jerusalem to visit Cephas, and remained with him fifteen days.* [19] *But I saw none of the other apostles except James the Lord's brother.* [20] *(In what I am writing to you, before God, I do not lie!)* [21] *Then I went into the regions of Syria and Cilicia.* [22] *And I was still not known by sight to the churches of Christ in Judea;* [23] *they only heard it said, 'He who once persecuted us is now preaching the faith he once tried to destroy.'* [24] *And they glorified God because of me.*

WE have seen in Galatians 1:6–10 that there is only one gospel, and that this gospel is the criterion by which all human opinions are to be tested. It is the gospel which Paul presented.

The question now is, what is the *origin* of Paul's gospel that it should be normative, and that other messages and opinions should be assessed and judged by it? Without doubt it is a very wonderful gospel. We think of the Epistle to the Romans, the Corinthian Epistles and those mighty prison Epistles like Ephesians, Philippians and Colossians. We are impressed by their majestic sweep, their profundity, their consistency, as Paul outlines the purpose of God from eternity to eternity. But where did Paul get it all from? Was it the product of his own fertile brain? Did he make it up? Or was it stale second-hand stuff with no original authority? Did he crib it from the other apostles in Jerusalem, which the Judaizers evidently maintained, as they tried to subordinate his authority to theirs?

Paul's answer to these questions may be found in verses 11 and 12: *For I would have you know, brethren,* (a favourite formula of his to introduce an important statement) *that the gospel which was preached by me is not man's gospel. For I did not receive it from man, nor was I taught it, but it came through a revelation of Jesus Christ.* The reason why Paul's gospel was the yardstick by which other gospels were to be measured is now clear. It is that his gospel was (literally, verse 11) 'not according to man'; it was 'no human invention' (JBP, NEB). 'I preached it,' Paul could say, 'but I did not invent it. Nor did I receive it from a man, as if it were already an accepted tradition handed down from a previous generation. Nor was I taught it, so that I had to learn it from human teachers.' Instead, 'it came through a revelation of Jesus Christ.' This probably means that it was revealed by Jesus Christ. Alternatively, the genitive could be objective, in which case Christ is the substance of the revelation, as in verse 16, rather than its author. Whichever way we take it, the general sense is plain. As in verse 1 he asserted the divine origin of his apostolic commission, so now he asserts the divine origin of his apostolic gospel. Neither his mission nor his message was derived from man; both came to him direct from God and Jesus Christ.

Paul's claim, then, is this. His gospel, which was being called in question by the Judaizers and deserted by the Galatians, was neither an invention (as if his own brain had fabricated it), nor a tradition (as if the church had handed it down to him), but a revelation (for God had made it known to him). As John Brown puts it: 'Jesus Christ took him under his own immediate tuition.'[1] This is why Paul dared to call the gospel he preached '*my* gospel' (*cf.* Rom. 16:25). It was not 'his' because he had made it up but because it had been uniquely revealed to him. The magnitude of his claim is remarkable. He is affirming that his message is not his message but God's message, that his gospel is not his gospel but God's gospel, that his words are not his words but God's words.

Having made this startling claim to a direct revelation from God without human means, Paul goes on to prove it from history, that is,

[1] Brown, p. 58.

from the facts of his own autobiography. The situation before his conversion, at his conversion and after his conversion were such that he clearly got his gospel not from any man, but direct from God. We shall look at these three situations in turn.

1. WHAT HAPPENED BEFORE HIS CONVERSION (verses 13, 14)

For you have heard of my former life in Judaism, how I persecuted the church of God violently and tried to destroy it; and I advanced in Judaism beyond many of my own age among my people, so extremely zealous was I for the traditions of my fathers. Here the apostle describes his pre-conversion state 'in Judaism', that is, 'when I was still a practising Jew' (NEB). What he had been like in those days was well known. 'You have heard of my former life,' he says, for he had told them. He mentions two aspects of his unregenerate days, his persecution of the church, which he now knew to be 'the church of God' (verse 13), and his enthusiasm for the traditions of his fathers (verse 14). In both, he says, he was fanatical.

Take his persecution of the church. Paul persecuted the church of God 'beyond measure' (AV). The phrase seems to indicate the violence, even the savagery, with which he set about this grim work. What he tells us here we can supplement from the book of Acts. He went from house to house in Jerusalem, seized any Christians he could find, men and women, and dragged them off to prison (Acts 8:3). When these Christians were put to death, he cast his vote against them (Acts 26:10). Not satisfied with *persecuting* the church, he was actually bent on *destroying* it (verse 13). He was determined to stamp it out.

He was equally fanatical in his enthusiasm for Jewish traditions. 'I was outstripping many of my Jewish contemporaries in my boundless devotion to the traditions of my ancestors,' he writes (verse 14, NEB). He had been brought up according to 'the strictest party' of the Jewish religion (Acts 26:5), namely as a Pharisee, and this is how he had lived.

Such was the state of Saul of Tarsus before his conversion. He was a bigot and a fanatic, whole-hearted in his devotion to Judaism and in his persecution of Christ and the church.

Now a man in that mental and emotional state is in no mood to change his mind, or even to have it changed for him by men. No conditioned reflex or other psychological device could convert a man in that state. Only God could reach him—and God did!

2. WHAT HAPPENED AT HIS CONVERSION (verses 15, 16a)

But when he who had set me apart before I was born, and had called me through his grace, was pleased to reveal his Son to me, in order that I might preach him among the Gentiles.... The contrast between verses 13 and 14 on the one hand and verses 15 and 16 on the other is dramatically abrupt. It is clearly seen in the subjects of the verbs. In verses 13 and 14, Paul is speaking about himself, '*I* persecuted the church of God . . . *I* tried to destroy it . . . *I* advanced in Judaism . . ., so extremely zealous was *I* for the traditions of my fathers.' But in verses 15 and 16 he begins to speak of God. It was *God*, he writes, who 'set me apart before I was born', *God* who 'called me through his grace', and *God* who 'was pleased to reveal his Son to me'. In other words, 'in my fanaticism I was bent upon a course of persecution and destruction, but God (whom I had left out of my calculations) arrested me and changed my headlong course. All my raging fanaticism was no match for the good pleasure of God.'

Notice how at each stage the initiative and the grace of God are emphasized. First, God *set me apart before I was born.* Like Jacob who was chosen before he was born, in preference to his twin Esau (*cf.* Rom. 9:10–13), and like Jeremiah who before he was born was appointed to be a prophet (Je. 1:5), so Paul, before he was born, was set apart to be an apostle. If he was thus consecrated an apostle before his birth, then plainly he had nothing to do with it himself.

Next, his pre-natal choice led to his historical call. God *called me through his grace*, that is, His utterly undeserved love. Paul was fighting against God, against Christ, against men. He neither deserved mercy, nor asked for it. Yet mercy found him, and grace called him.

Thirdly, God *was pleased to reveal his Son to me.* Whether Paul is still referring to his experience on the Damascus road or to the days immediately following it, what was revealed to him was Jesus Christ, God's Son. Paul had been persecuting Christ, because he believed that Jesus Christ was an impostor. Now his eyes were opened to see Jesus not as a mountebank but as the Messiah of the

Jews, the Son of God and the Saviour of the world. He already knew some of the facts about Jesus (he is not claiming that these were revealed to him supernaturally, either then or later, *cf.* 1 Cor. 11:23), but now he grasped their significance. It was a revelation of Christ for the Gentiles, for God 'was pleased to reveal his Son to me, in order that I might preach him among the Gentiles'. It was a private revelation to Paul, but it was for a public communication to the Gentiles. *Cf.* Acts 9:15. And what Paul was charged to preach to the Gentiles was not the law of Moses, as the Judaizers were teaching, but good news (the meaning of the verb 'preach' in verse 16)—the good news of Christ. This Christ had been revealed, Paul says, 'in me' (literally). We know that it was an external unveiling, for Paul claimed that he saw the risen Christ (*e.g.* 1 Cor. 9:1; 15:8, 9). Yet essentially it was an inner illumination of his soul, God shining into his heart 'to give the light of the knowledge of the glory of God in the face of Christ' (2 Cor. 4:6). And this revelation was so inward, and became so much a part of him, that he was able to make it known to others. Hence the New English Bible phrase 'to reveal his Son to me and through me'.

The thrust of these verses is very compelling. Saul of Tarsus had been a fanatical opponent of the gospel. But it pleased God to make him a preacher of the very gospel he had been so bitterly opposing. His pre-natal choice, his historical call and the revelation of Christ in him were all the work of God. Therefore, neither his apostolic mission nor his message came from men.

However, the apostle's argument is not yet complete. Granted that his conversion was a work of God, as is plain from how it happened and what preceded it, did he not receive instruction *after* his conversion, so that his message was, after all, from men? No. This too Paul denies.

3. WHAT HAPPENED AFTER HIS CONVERSION (verses 16b–24)

I did not confer with flesh and blood, nor did I go up to Jerusalem to those who were apostles before me, but I went away into Arabia; and again I returned to Damascus. Then after three years I went up to Jerusalem to visit Cephas, and remained with him fifteen days. But I saw none of the other apostles except James the Lord's brother. (In what I am writing to you, before God, I do not lie!) Then I went into the regions of Syria and Cilicia. And I was still not known by sight to the churches of Christ in Judea; they only heard it said, 'He who once persecuted us is now preaching the faith he once tried to destroy.' And they glorified God because of me.

In this rather longer paragraph the emphatic statement is the first, at the end of verse 16, 'I did not confer with flesh and blood.' That is, Paul says that he did not consult any human being. We know that Ananias came to him, but evidently Paul did not discuss the gospel with him, nor with any of the Jerusalem apostles. He now elaborates this statement historically. He produces a series of three alibis to prove that he did not spend time in Jerusalem, having his gospel shaped by the other apostles.

Alibi 1. He went into Arabia (verse 17)

According to Acts 9:20 Paul spent a little while in Damascus preaching, which suggests that his gospel was already clearly enough defined for him to announce it. But it must have been soon afterwards that he went into Arabia. Bishop Lightfoot comments: 'A veil of thick darkness hangs over St. Paul's visit to Arabia.'[1] We know neither where he went nor why he went there. Possibly it was not far from Damascus, because the whole district at that time was ruled by King Aretas of Arabia. Some people think he went into Arabia as a missionary to preach the gospel. St. Chrysostom describes 'a barbarous and savage people'[2] who lived there, whom Paul went to evangelize. But it is much more likely that he went into Arabia for quiet and solitude, for this is the point of verses 16 and 17, 'I did not confer with flesh and blood . . . but I went away into Arabia.' He seems to have stayed there for three years (verse 18). We believe that in this period of withdrawal, as he meditated on the Old Testament Scriptures, on the facts of the life and death of Jesus that he already knew and on his experience of conversion, the gospel of the grace of God was revealed to him in its fullness. It has even been suggested that those three years in Arabia were a deliberate compensation for the three years of instruction which Jesus gave the other apostles, but which Paul missed. Now he had Jesus to himself, as it were, for three years of solitude in the wilderness.

[1] Lightfoot, p. 87. [2] Quoted by Lightfoot, p. 90.

Alibi 2. He went up to Jerusalem later and briefly (verses 18–20)

The occasion is probably that referred to in Acts 9:26, after he had been smuggled out of Damascus, being lowered down the city wall in a basket. Paul is quite open about this visit to Jerusalem, but he makes light of it. It was not nearly as significant as the false teachers were obviously suggesting. Several features of it are mentioned.

For one thing, it took place 'after three years' (verse 18). This almost certainly means three years after his conversion, by which time his gospel would have been fully formulated.

Next, when he reached Jerusalem, he saw only two of the apostles, Peter and James. He went 'to see' (AV) or 'to visit' (RSV) Peter. The Greek verb (*historēsai*) was used of sight-seeing, and means 'to visit for the purpose of coming to know somebody' (Arndt-Gingrich), Luther comments that he went to these apostles 'not commanded, but of his own accord, not to learn anything of them, but only to see Peter'.[1] Paul also saw James, who seems here to be numbered among the apostles (verse 19). But he did not see any of the other apostles. They may have been absent, or too busy, or even frightened of him (*cf.* Acts 9:26).

Thirdly, he was in Jerusalem for only 'fifteen days'. Of course in fifteen days the apostles would have had some time to talk about Christ. But Paul's point is that he had no time in a fortnight to absorb from Peter the whole counsel of God. Besides, that was not the purpose of his visit. Much of those two weeks in Jerusalem, we learn from Acts (9:28, 29), was spent in preaching.

To sum up, Paul's first visit to Jerusalem was only after three years, it lasted only two weeks, and he saw only two apostles. It was, therefore, ludicrous to suggest that he obtained his gospel from the Jerusalem apostles.

Alibi 3. He went off to Syria and Cilicia (verses 20–24)

This visit to the extreme north corresponds to Acts 9:30 where we are told that Paul, who was already in danger for his life, was brought by the brethren to Caesarea, where they 'sent him off to Tarsus', which is in Cilicia. Since he says here that he 'went into

[1] Luther, p. 87.

the regions of Syria' as well, he may have revisited Damascus and called at Antioch on his way to Tarsus. Be that as it may, the point Paul is making is that he was up in the far north, nowhere near Jerusalem.

As a result, he 'was still not known by sight to the churches of Christ in Judea' (verse 22). They only knew him by hearsay, and the rumour they had heard was that their erstwhile persecutor had turned preacher (verse 23). Indeed, he had become a preacher of 'the faith' which they had accepted and which previously he had 'tried to destroy'. Learning this, 'they glorified God because of me'. They did not glorify Paul, but God in Paul, recognizing that Paul was a signal trophy of God's grace.

Not until fourteen years later (2:1), presumably meaning fourteen years after his conversion, did Paul revisit Jerusalem and have a more prolonged consultation with the other apostles. By that time his gospel was fully developed. But during the fourteen-year period between his conversion and this consultation he had paid only one brief and insignificant visit to Jerusalem. The rest of the time he had spent in distant Arabia, Syria and Cilicia. His alibis proved the independence of his gospel.

What Paul has been saying in verses 13 to 24 may be summarized thus: The fanaticism of his pre-conversion career, the divine initiative in his conversion, and his almost total isolation from the Jerusalem church leaders afterwards together combined to demonstrate that his message was not from man but from God. Further, this historical, circumstantial evidence could not be gainsaid. The apostle is able to confirm and guarantee it by a solemn affirmation: 'In what I am writing to you, before God, I do not lie!' (verse 20).

CONCLUSION

We return, in conclusion, to the assertion which these autobiographical details have been marshalled to establish. Verses 11 and 12: *For I would have you know, brethren, that the gospel which was preached by me is not man's gospel. For I did not receive it from man, nor was I taught it, but it came through a revelation of Jesus Christ.* Having considered Paul's lack of contact with the Jerusalem apostles during the first fourteen years of his apostolate, can we accept the divine origin of his message? Many do not.

Some people admire Paul's massive intellect, but find his teaching harsh, dry and complicated; so they reject it.

Others say that Paul was responsible for corrupting the simple Christianity of Jesus Christ. It was fashionable about a century ago to drive a wedge between Jesus and Paul. It is generally recognized nowadays, however, that you cannot do this, for all the seeds of Paul's theology are to be found in the teaching of Jesus. Nevertheless the 'wedge theory' still has its advocates. For example, Lord Beaverbrook wrote a little life of Christ which he called *The Divine Propagandist.* He tells us that he wrote it 'as a man of affairs', and that he was 'trying to understand Jesus in the flickering light of a limited intelligence and certainly restricted research'. 'I have searched the gospels and neglected theology,' he says. His theme is that the church has much misunderstood and misrepresented Jesus Christ. As for the apostle Paul, Lord Beaverbrook's opinion is that he was 'incapable by nature of understanding the spirit of the Master'. He 'did damage to Christianity and left his imprint by wiping out many of the traces of the footsteps of his Master'.[1] But Paul cannot have misrepresented Christ if he was communicating a special revelation of Christ, which is what he claims in Galatians 1.

Other people take the view that Paul was just an ordinary man, sharing our passions and our fallibility, so that his opinion is no better than anybody else's. But Paul says his message is not according to man but from Jesus Christ.

Yet others say that Paul simply reflected the view of the first-century Christian community. But Paul is at pains in this passage to show that his authorization was not ecclesiastical. He was totally independent of the church leaders. He got his views from Christ, not from the church.

This, then, is our dilemma. Are we to accept Paul's account of the origin of his message, supported as it is by solid historical evidence? Or shall we prefer our own theory, although supported by no historical evidence? If Paul was right in asserting that his gospel was not man's but God's (*cf.* Rom. 1:1), then to reject Paul is to reject God.

[1] *The Divine Propagandist*, by Lord Beaverbrook (Heinemann, 1962), pp. 11, 12.

2:1–10

ONLY ONE GOSPEL

THEN after fourteen years I went up again to Jerusalem with Barnabas, taking Titus along with me. [2] I went up by revelation; and I laid before them (but privately before those who were of repute) the gospel which I preach among the Gentiles, lest somehow I should be running or had run in vain. [3] But even Titus, who was with me, was not compelled to be circumcised, though he was a Greek. [4] But because of false brethren secretly brought in, who slipped in to spy out our freedom which we have in Christ Jesus, that they might bring us into bondage—[5] to them we did not yield submission even for a moment, that the truth of the gospel might be preserved for you. [6] And from those who were reputed to be something (what they were makes no difference to me; God shows no partiality)—those, I say, who were of repute added nothing to me; [7] but on the contrary, when they saw that I had been entrusted with the gospel to the uncircumcised, just as Peter had been entrusted with the gospel to the circumcised [8] (for he who worked through Peter for the mission to the circumcised worked through me also for the Gentiles), [9] and when they perceived the grace that was given to me, James and Cephas and John, who were reputed to be pillars, gave to me and Barnabas the right hand of fellowship, that we should go to the Gentiles and they to the circumcised; [10] only they would have us remember the poor, which very thing I was eager to do.

THE bane of Paul's life and ministry was the insidious activity of false teachers. Wherever he went, they dogged his footsteps. No sooner had he planted the gospel in some locality, than false teachers began to trouble the church by perverting it. Further, as we have seen, in order to discredit Paul's message, they also challenged his authority.

This matter is of importance for us because Paul's detractors have plenty of successors in the Christian church today. They tell us that we do not need to pay too much attention to his writings. They forget or deny that he was an apostle of Jesus Christ, uniquely called, commissioned, authorized and inspired to teach in His name. They ignore Paul's own claim (1:11, 12) that he derived his gospel not from men but from Jesus Christ.

One of the ways in which some false teachers of Paul's day tried to undermine his authority was to hint that his gospel was different from Peter's, and indeed from the views of all the other apostles in Jerusalem. 'As a result', they said, 'the church is being saddled with two gospels, Paul's and Peter's, each claiming a divine origin. Which are we going to accept?' 'Surely', they went on, 'we cannot follow Paul if he is in a minority of one, and if Peter and the rest of the apostles disagree with him?' This was evidently one of the specious arguments of the Judaizers. They were trying to disrupt the unity of the apostolic circle. They were openly alleging that the apostles contradicted one another. Their game, we might say, was not 'robbing Peter to pay Paul', but exalting Peter to spite Paul!

To this insinuation Paul now addresses himself. He has shown in chapter 1 that his gospel came from God not man. He now shows in the first part of chapter 2 that his gospel was precisely the same as that of the other apostles; it was not different. To prove that his gospel was independent of the other apostles, he has stressed that he paid only one visit to Jerusalem in fourteen years, and that this lasted only fifteen days. To prove that his gospel was yet identical with theirs, he now stresses that when he paid a proper visit to Jerusalem, his gospel was endorsed and approved by them.

Let us consider the circumstances of this visit to Jerusalem. Verses 1 and 2: *Then after fourteen years I went up again to Jerusalem with Barnabas, taking Titus along with me. I went up by revelation; and I laid before them (but privately before those who were of repute) the gospel which I preach among the Gentiles, lest somehow I should be running or had run in vain.*

This was his second visit ('I went up again'), and it was 'after fourteen years' (dating probably from his conversion, not from his first visit). There are two important aspects of this visit, namely his companions and his message.

First, his *companions.* These were Barnabas and Titus. What is particularly remarkable about that is that Barnabas was a Jew (although he was associated with Paul in his mission to the Gentiles in Antioch and later on the first missionary journey), whereas Titus was a Greek. That is, Titus was an uncircumcised Gentile, himself a product of the very Gentile mission which was then in dispute and which the Judaizers were challenging.

Second, his *gospel*. Paul's gospel, which he preached to the Gentiles, he now laid before the other apostles. True, this was not his reason for going to Jerusalem. The occasion of his visit was different. He 'went up by revelation', he says (verse 2). That is to say, he went up because God told him to go, not because the Jerusalem apostles had sent for him to put him on the mat. (What this revelation was we do not know, but the reference may be to Agabus' prophecy of a famine, as a result of which Paul and Barnabas were sent to Jerusalem on a relief mission. *Cf.* Acts 11:27–30.) True also, the consultation between Paul and the other apostles was a small and private affair. It was not in any sense an official conference or 'synod'.

Nevertheless, although it was neither the purpose of his visit to Jerusalem nor an official arrangement, this consultation did take place. In it, Paul 'laid before' the Jerusalem apostles the gospel that he was preaching to the Gentiles, and he says he did it 'lest somehow I should be running or had run in vain'. It was not, we may be sure, that he had any personal doubts or misgivings about his gospel and needed the reassurance of the other Jerusalem apostles, for he had been preaching it for fourteen years; but rather lest his ministry, past and present, should be rendered fruitless by the Judaizers. It was to overthrow their influence, not to strengthen his own conviction, that he laid his gospel before the Jerusalem apostles.

Such were the two vital features of his visit. He took with him to Jerusalem a Gentile companion and a Gentile gospel. It was a tense and crucial situation, an occasion fraught with great peril and equally great possibility for the subsequent history of the Christian church. What would be the reaction of the apostles in Jerusalem to Paul's Gentile companion and Gentile mission? Would they receive Titus as a brother or repudiate him because he was uncircumcised? Would they endorse Paul's gospel or attempt to modify it in some way? These were the questions in everybody's mind. Behind them was the fundamental question: would the liberty with which Christ has made us free be maintained, or would the church be condemned to bondage and sterility? Had the Judaizers any ground for their rumour that there was a rift in the ranks of the apostles?

Paul tells his readers what happened at that epoch-making

consultation. His Gentile companion Titus was not compelled to be circumcised (verses 3–5), and his Gentile gospel was not contradicted or even modified in any way (verses 6–10). On the contrary, Titus was accepted, and Paul's gospel was accepted also. Thus a great and resounding victory was won for the truth of the gospel. The rift in the apostolic ranks was a myth; there was no substance to it.

Having introduced the main thrust of the argument in these verses, we must now examine them in greater detail.

1. PAUL'S COMPANION (verses 3–5)

But even Titus, who was with me, was not compelled to be circumcised, though he was a Greek. But because of false brethren secretly brought in, who slipped in to spy out our freedom which we have in Christ Jesus, that they might bring us into bondage—to them we did not yield submission even for a moment, that the truth of the gospel might be preserved for you.

Of course, it was a daring step of Paul's to take Titus with him at all. Thus to introduce a Gentile into the headquarters of the Jerusalem church could have been interpreted as a deliberate act of provocation. In a sense, it probably was, although Paul's motive was not provocative. It was not in order to stir up strife that he brought Titus with him to Jerusalem, but in order to establish the truth of the gospel. This truth is that Jews and Gentiles are accepted by God on the same terms, namely through faith in Jesus Christ, and must therefore be accepted by the church without any discrimination between them.

Such was the issue. And in the event, the point was made and the truth established: 'Titus . . . was not compelled to be circumcised, though he was a Greek.' However, the victory was not won without a battle, for strong pressure was exerted on Paul to circumcise Titus. This came from 'false brethren', whom the New English Bible calls 'sham-Christians' and J. B. Phillips 'pseudo-Christians'. As John Brown judiciously comments, 'These persons were brethren, *i.e.* Christians in name; but they were "False brethren", Jews in reality.'[1] They were almost certainly Judaizers, and Paul has some stern words to say about them. They were intruders, 'interlopers' (NEB). This may mean either that they had no business

[1] Brown, p. 75.

to be in the church fellowship at all, or that they had gate-crashed the private conference with the apostles. So J. B. Phillips understands it, translating 'who wormed their way into our meeting'. In either case, in Paul's view they were spies. They had 'slipped in to spy out our freedom which we have in Christ Jesus, that they might bring us into bondage'. In particular, they tried to insist on Titus being circumcised. We know that this was the platform of the Judaizing party, for their slogan is given us in Acts 15:1: 'Unless you are circumcised according to the custom of Moses, you cannot be saved.'

Paul saw the issue plainly. It was not just a question of circumcision and uncircumcision, of Gentile and Jewish customs. It was a matter of fundamental importance regarding the truth of the gospel, namely, of Christian freedom versus bondage. The Christian has been set free from the law in the sense that his acceptance before God depends entirely upon God's grace in the death of Jesus Christ received by faith. To introduce the works of the law and make our acceptance depend on our obedience to rules and regulations was to bring a free man into bondage again. Of this principle Titus was a test case. It is true that he was an uncircumcised Gentile, but he was a converted Christian. Having believed in Jesus, he had been accepted by God in Christ, and that, Paul said, was enough. Nothing further was necessary for his salvation, as the Council of Jerusalem was later to confirm (see Acts 15).

So Paul stood firm. 'The truth of the gospel' was at stake, and he was determined at all costs to maintain it. He resisted the pressure of the Judaizers, and the apostles did not compel Titus to be circumcised. 'To them (that is, the false brethren) we did not yield submission even for a moment' (verse 5). Or, 'not for one moment did I yield to their dictation' (NEB).

It is necessary to add that these verses could be interpreted, and are interpreted by some commentators, in such a way as to understand that Paul gave in and that Titus was circumcised. Bishop Lightfoot refers to the paragraph as 'this shipwreck of grammar'.[1] Paul is evidently writing under the stress of strong emotion, even of considerable embarrassment. He leaves his sentence in verse 4 unfinished, and we can only guess what he would have said if he had completed it. Further, although all the great Greek codices include

[1] Lightfoot, p. 104.

the negative in verse 5 ('we did *not* yield submission'), there are one or two Latin versions which omit it. This is reflected in the margin of the New English Bible: 'I yielded to their demand for the moment.' It seems right to reject this reading, as do both the Revised Standard Version and the New English Bible. But if by chance it is correct, then we must understand that Paul circumcised Titus, as he later circumcised Timothy, as a conciliatory gesture (Acts 16:3). Once a vital principle of gospel truth had been established, Paul was willing to make policy concessions. But, he insists here, he did it voluntarily, not out of compulsion. For, whether Titus was circumcised or not, verse 3 stands: 'Titus . . . was not *compelled* to be circumcised.' So does verse 5b, that Paul's motive was to preserve 'the truth of the gospel'. However, my own belief is that the RSV and NEB texts are right, and that Titus was not circumcised. As Bishop Lightfoot very properly points out, the people to whom Paul made concessions were *weak* brethren, not *false*.[1]

2. PAUL'S GOSPEL (verses 6–9a)

As we have already seen, Paul had a private interview with the Jerusalem apostles (verse 2). We know who these men were, before whom he laid his gospel, because they are identified by name later in verse 9. They are James, the Lord's brother, Peter and John. In other verses in this paragraph, however, Paul uses indirect expressions to describe them. They are 'the men of repute' (verse 2, NEB), those 'reputed to be something' (verse 6) and those 'reputed to be pillars' (verse 9). In each case Paul alludes to them according to their repute. He is not being derogatory to them, for he has acknowledged them already in Galatians 1:17 as 'apostles before me', and he is to tell us in verse 9 that they gave him 'the right hand of fellowship'. Why then does he refer to them in this roundabout way? Probably his expressions were influenced by the fact that the Judaizers were exaggerating the status of the Jerusalem apostles at the expense of his own. As Lightfoot puts it, Paul was 'depreciatory not indeed of the Twelve themselves, but of the extravagant and exclusive claims set up for them by the Judaizers'.[2]

Perhaps the false brethren were drawing attention to what they

[1] Lightfoot, p. 106. [2] Lightfoot, p. 108.

regarded as the superior qualifications of James, Peter and John—that James was one of the Lord's brethren, and that Peter and John had belonged to the inner circle of three. Besides this, they had of course known Jesus in the days of His flesh, which Paul probably had not. It may be to this that Paul refers in the parenthesis of verse 6: 'what they *were* makes no difference to me; God shows no partiality.' Or 'God does not recognize these personal distinctions' (NEB). Paul's words are neither a denial of, nor a mark of disrespect for, their apostolic authority. He is simply indicating that, although he accepts their *office* as apostles, he is not overawed by their *person* as it was being inflated by the Judaizers.

3. THE OUTCOME OF THE CONSULTATION (verses 9b, 10)

Here, then, is Paul laying his gospel before the Jerusalem apostles. What was the outcome of this consultation? Did they contradict his gospel? Did they modify it, edit it, trim it, supplement it? No. Paul mentions two results, one negative and the other positive.

The negative outcome is seen at the end of verse 6: they *added nothing to me*. In other words, they did not find Paul's gospel defective. They made no attempt to add circumcision to it, or to embellish it in any other way. They did not say to Paul, 'Your gospel is all right as far as it goes, but it does not go far enough; you must add to it.' In fact, they changed nothing. Significantly, Paul describes the gospel which he laid before the apostles as 'the gospel which I preach' (present tense). It is as if he wrote: 'the gospel which I submitted to the other apostles is the gospel which I am still preaching. The gospel which I am preaching today was not altered by them. It is the same as I preached before I saw them. It is the gospel which I preached to you and which you received. I have added nothing, subtracted nothing, changed nothing. It is you Galatians who are deserting the gospel; it is not I.' This, then, was the negative result. They 'added nothing to me'.

The positive outcome of the consultation was that they *gave to me ... the right hand of fellowship* (verse 9). They recognized that they and Paul had been entrusted with the same gospel. The only difference between them was that they had been allocated different spheres in which to preach it. The Authorized Version rendering of verse 7 is a little misleading. It refers to 'the gospel of the uncircumcision' and 'the gospel of the circumcision', as if they were two different gospels, one for the Gentiles and one for the Jews. This is not so. What the apostles realized was that God was at work in His grace through both Peter and Paul (verses 8, 9). So they gave Paul the right hand of fellowship, which means that they 'accepted Barnabas and myself as partners, and shook hands upon it' (NEB). They simply recognized *that we should go to the Gentiles and they to the circumcised* (verse 9).

They also added that they wanted Paul and Barnabas to *remember the poor*, the poverty-stricken churches of Judea, which, Paul says, was the *very thing I was eager to do* (verse 10). Indeed, it was primarily for famine relief that he and Barnabas were in Jerusalem at that time, as we saw earlier. And he continued to care for the poor in the following years, organizing his famous collection. He urged the more wealthy Gentile churches of Macedonia and Achaia to support the poorer churches of Judea, and regarded their gift as a means to foster and demonstrate Jewish–Gentile solidarity in the fellowship of the Christian church.

Looking back over the first paragraph of Galatians 2, we have learnt that, on his second visit to Jerusalem, Paul met two groups of men, whose attitude to him differed completely. The 'false brethren', who disagreed with his gospel and his policy, tried to compel Titus to be circumcised. Paul refused to submit to them. The apostles, on the other hand, acknowledged the truth of Paul's gospel and gave him their hand in confirmation.

CONCLUSION

Some people who read these pages will no doubt be tempted to be impatient. It seems to them no more than a complicated rigmarole. A visit of Paul to Jerusalem in the first century AD, the question of whether Titus was circumcised or not, a consultation between Paul and the Jerusalem apostles—it all appears very remote and quite unrelated to twentieth-century problems. But this is not so. At least two principles of the utmost importance emerge from this paragraph.

a. The truth of the gospel is one and unchanging

We saw, when we were considering Galatians 1:6–10, that there is only one gospel. We can now elaborate and say that the whole New

Testament presents this one gospel consistently. It is fashionable in some quarters to talk about the 'Pauline' gospel and the 'Petrine' gospel and the 'Johannine' gospel, as if they were quite different from one another. Some people refer to 'Paulinism', as if it were a distinctive brand of Christianity, even a different religion altogether. And sometimes people set Paul and James over against each other as if they contradicted each other.

But all this is mistaken. The apostles of Jesus Christ do not contradict one another in the New Testament. Certainly, there are differences of *style* between them, because their inspiration did not obliterate their individual personality. There are also differences of *emphasis*, because they were called to different spheres and preached or wrote to different audiences. Consequently, they stressed different aspects of the gospel. For example, Paul was writing against legalists and James against antinomians. But they complement one another. There is only one gospel, the apostolic faith, a recognizable body of doctrine taught by the apostles of Jesus Christ and preserved for us in the New Testament. Paul is at pains in this passage to show that he was in full agreement with the Jerusalem apostles and they with him. He makes the same point in 1 Corinthians 15:11: 'whether then it was I or they, so we preach and so you believed.' There is only one New Testament gospel, only one Christianity; there are not several different legitimate alternatives.

It is still so today. If there is only one gospel in the New Testament, there is only one gospel for the church. The gospel has not changed with the changing centuries. Whether it is preached to young or old, to east or west, to Jews or Gentiles, to cultured or uncultured, to scientists or non-scientists, although its presentation may vary, its substance is the same. Paul and Peter had a different commission, but they had a common message.

b. The truth of the gospel must be maintained

This is the second principle which is illustrated in Galatians 2. Paul was determined to resist these Judaizers. He was even prepared, as we shall see in the next paragraph (verses 11–14), to oppose Peter to his face when his conduct contradicted the gospel. Paul was very gentle with 'weak' brethren, whose conscience was over-scrupulous. He was ready to make policy concessions, as when he later circumcised Timothy. But on a matter of principle, when the truth of the gospel was at stake, he stood firm and would not budge.

This combination of softness and strength is well expressed by Martin Luther: 'Let this be then the conclusion of all together, that we will suffer our goods to be taken away, our name, our life, and all that we have; but the Gospel, our faith, Jesus Christ, we will never suffer to be wrested from us. And cursed be that humility which here abaseth and submitteth itself. Nay rather, let every Christian man here be proud and spare not, except he will deny Christ.

'Wherefore, God assisting me, my forehead shall be more hard than all men's foreheads. Here I take upon me this title, according to the proverb: *cedo nulli*, I give place to none. Yea, I am glad even with all my heart, in this point to seem rebellious and obstinate. And here I confess that I am and ever will be stout and stern, and will not one inch give place to any creature. Charity giveth place, for it "beareth all things, believeth all things, hopeth all things, endureth all things" (1 Cor. 13:7), but faith giveth no place. . . .

'Now, as concerning faith we ought to be invincible, and more hard, if it might be, than the adamant stone; but as touching charity, we ought to be soft, and more flexible than the reed or leaf that is shaken with the wind, and ready to yield to everything.'[1]

[1] Luther, pp. 108, 111, 112.

2:11–16

PAUL CLASHES WITH PETER IN ANTIOCH

BUT *when Cephas came to Antioch I opposed him to his face, because he stood condemned.* [12] *For before certain men came from James, he ate with the Gentiles; but when they came he drew back and separated himself, fearing the circumcision party.* [13] *And with him the rest of the Jews acted insincerely, so that even Barnabas was carried away by their insincerity.* [14] *But when I saw that they were not straightforward about the truth of the gospel, I said to Cephas before them all, 'If you, though a Jew, live like a Gentile and not like a Jew, how can you compel the Gentiles to live like Jews?'* [15] *We ourselves, who are Jews by birth and not Gentile sinners,* [16] *yet who know that a man is not justified by works of the law but through faith in Jesus Christ, even we have believed in Christ Jesus, in order to be justified by faith in Christ, and not by works of the law, because by works of the law shall no one be justified.*

THIS is without doubt one of the most tense and dramatic episodes in the New Testament. Here are two leading apostles of Jesus Christ face to face in complete and open conflict.

The scene has changed from Jerusalem, the capital of Jewry, to which the early verses of this chapter belong, to Antioch, the chief city of Syria, even of Asia, where the Gentile mission began, and where the disciples were first called 'Christians'. When Paul visited Jerusalem, Peter (together with James and John) gave him the right hand of fellowship (verses 1–10). When Peter visited Antioch, Paul opposed him to the face (verses 11–16).

Now both Paul and Peter were Christian men, men of God, who knew what it is to be forgiven through Christ and to have received the Holy Spirit. Further, they were both apostles of Jesus Christ, specially called, commissioned and invested with authority by Him. They were both honoured in the churches for their leadership. They had both been mightily used by God. In fact, the book of Acts is virtually divided in half by them, the first part telling the story of Peter and the second part the story of Paul.

Yet here is the apostle Paul opposing the apostle Peter to his face, contradicting him, rebuking him, condemning him, because he had withdrawn and separated himself from Gentile Christian believers, and would no longer eat with them. It was not that Peter denied the gospel in his *teaching*, for Paul has been at pains to show that he and the Jerusalem apostles were at one in their understanding of the gospel (verses 1–10), and he repeats this fact here (verses 14–16). Peter's offence against the gospel was in his *conduct*. In J. B. Phillips' words, his 'behaviour was a contradiction of the truth of the gospel'.

We must investigate this situation, in which these two leading apostles were at loggerheads. In particular, it is important to note what each apostle did, why he did it and with what result. We shall begin with Peter.

1. THE CONDUCT OF PETER (verses 11–13)

a. What he did

When Peter first arrived in Antioch, he ate with Gentile Christians. Indeed, the imperfect tense of the verb shows that this had been his regular practice. 'He . . . was in the habit of eating his meals with the gentiles' (JBP). His old Jewish scruples had been overcome. He did not consider himself in any way defiled or contaminated by contact with uncircumcised Gentile Christians, as once he would have done. Instead, he welcomed them to eat with him, and he ate with them. Peter, who was a Jewish Christian, enjoyed table-fellowship with the Antiochene believers, who were Gentile Christians. This probably means that they had ordinary meals together, although doubtless they partook together of the Lord's Supper as well.

Then one day a group arrived in Antioch from Jerusalem. They were all professing Christian believers, but they were Jewish in origin, indeed strict Pharisees (Acts 15:5). They came 'from James' (Gal. 2:12), the leader of the Jerusalem church. This does not mean that they had his authority, for he later denied this (Acts 15:24), but rather that they *claimed* to have it. They posed as apostolic delegates.

On arrival in Antioch they began to preach: 'Unless you are circumcised according to the custom of Moses, you cannot be saved' (Acts 15:1). Evidently they went even further than that and taught that it was improper for circumcised Jewish believers to have table-fellowship with uncircumcised Gentile believers, even though the latter had believed in Jesus and been baptized.

These Judaizing teachers won a notable convert to their pernicious policy in the person of the apostle Peter. For Peter, who had previously eaten with these Gentile Christians, now withdrew from them and separated himself. He seems to have taken this action shamefacedly. As Bishop Lightfoot says, 'the words describe forcibly the cautious withdrawal of a timid person who shrinks from observation'.[1]

b. Why he did it

Why did Peter create this disastrous breach in the fellowship of the church in Antioch? We have already seen the immediate cause, namely that 'certain men came from James' (verse 12). But why did he give in to them? Are we to suppose that they convinced him that he had been doing wrong to eat with Gentile Christians? This cannot be so.

Let me remind you that only a short while previously, as is recorded in Acts 10 and 11, Peter had been granted a direct, special revelation from God on this very subject. He had been on the roof-top of a house in Joppa one afternoon when he fell into a trance. He saw in his vision a sheet let down from heaven by its four corners, containing an assortment of unclean creatures (birds, beasts and reptiles). He then heard a voice saying to him: 'Rise, Peter; kill and eat.' When he objected, the voice went on: 'What God has cleansed, you must not call common.' The vision was repeated three times for emphasis. From it Peter concluded that he must accompany the Gentile messengers who had come from the centurion Cornelius and enter his house, which action was unlawful for him as a Jew. In the sermon that he preached to Cornelius' household he said: 'Truly I perceive that God shows no partiality.' When the Holy Spirit fell upon the Gentiles who believed, Peter agreed that they must receive Christian baptism and be welcomed into the Christian church.

[1] Lightfoot, p. 112.

Are we to suppose that Peter had now forgotten the vision at Joppa and the conversion of the household of Cornelius? Or that he now went back on the revelation that God had given him then? Surely not. There is no suggestion in Galatians 2 that Peter had changed his mind. Why then did he withdraw from fellowship with Gentile believers in Antioch? Paul tells us. He 'separated himself, fearing the circumcision party' (verse 12). 'And with him the rest of the Jews acted insincerely, so that even Barnabas was carried away by their insincerity' (verse 13). The Greek word for 'insincerity' is 'hypocrisy', which means 'play-acting'. This is what they were doing. They 'played false' (NEB).

Paul's charge is serious, but plain. It is that Peter and the others acted in insincerity, and not from personal conviction. Their withdrawal from table-fellowship with Gentile believers was not prompted by any theological principle, but by craven fear of a small pressure group. In fact, Peter did in Antioch precisely what Paul had refused to do in Jerusalem, namely yield to pressure. The same Peter who had denied his Lord for fear of a maidservant now denied Him again for fear of the circumcision party. He still believed the gospel, but he failed to practise it. His conduct 'did not square' with it (NEB). He virtually contradicted it by his action, because he lacked the courage of his convictions.

c. What happened as a result

We have already noticed that 'the rest of the Jews acted insincerely, so that even Barnabas was carried away by their insincerity' (verse 13). 'Their dissimulation', comments Lightfoot, 'was as a flood which swept everything away with it.'[1] Even Barnabas, Paul's trusted friend and missionary colleague, who had stood firm with him in Jerusalem (verses 1, 9), now gave way in Antioch. This is important. If Paul had not taken his stand against Peter that day, either the whole Christian church would have drifted into a Jewish backwater and stagnated, or there would have been a permanent rift between Gentile and Jewish Christendom, 'one Lord, but two Lord's tables'.[2] Paul's outstanding courage on that occasion in

[1] Lightfoot, p. 113.
[2] Neill, p. 32.

resisting Peter preserved both the truth of the gospel and the international brotherhood of the church.

Now we leave Peter and turn to Paul.

2. THE CONDUCT OF PAUL (verses 14–16)

a. What he did

Verse 11: Paul 'withstood' (AV) or 'opposed' (RSV) Peter 'to his face'. The reason for Paul's drastic action was that Peter 'stood condemned'. That is to say, 'he was clearly in the wrong' (NEB). Not only so, but Paul rebuked Peter 'before them all' (verse 14), openly and publicly.

Paul did not hesitate out of deference for who Peter was. He recognized Peter as an apostle of Jesus Christ, who had indeed been appointed as an apostle before him (1:17). He knew that Peter was one of the 'pillars' of the church (verse 9), to whom God had entrusted the gospel to the circumcised (verse 7). Paul neither denied nor forgot these things. Nevertheless, this did not stop him from contradicting and opposing Peter. Nor did he shrink from doing it publicly. He did not listen to those who may well have counselled him to be cautious and to avoid washing dirty theological linen in public. He made no attempt to hush the dispute up or arrange (as we might) for a private discussion from which the public or the press were excluded. The consultation in Jerusalem had been private (verse 2), but the showdown in Antioch must be public. Peter's withdrawal from the Gentile believers had caused a public scandal; he had to be opposed in public too. So Paul's opposition to Peter was both 'to his face' (verse 11) and 'before them all' (verse 14). It was just the kind of open head-on collision which the church would seek at any price to avoid today.

b. Why he did it

How is it that Paul dared to contradict a fellow-apostle of Jesus Christ, and to do it publicly? Was it because he had an irascible disposition and could not control his temper or his tongue? Was he an exhibitionist, who enjoyed an argument? Did he regard Peter as a dangerous rival, so that he leapt at the opportunity to down him? No. None of these base passions motivated Paul.

Why then did he do it? The answer is simple. Paul acted as he did out of a deep concern for the very principle which Peter lacked. He knew that the theological principle at stake was no trivial matter. Martin Luther grasps this admirably: 'he hath here no trifling matter in hand, but the chiefest article of all Christian doctrine. . . . For what is Peter? What is Paul? What is an angel from heaven? What are all other creatures to the article of justification? Which if we know, then are we in the clear light; but if we be ignorant thereof, then are we in most miserable darkness.'[1]

What was this theological principle that was at stake? Twice in this chapter the apostle calls it 'the truth of the gospel'. This was the issue in Jerusalem (verse 5), and this was the issue again in Antioch (verse 14). Paul 'saw' this. Notice the spiritual perception into the fundamental issue which he claims—that Peter and the others were not 'walking straight' (literally, verse 14) according to the truth of the gospel. 'The truth of the gospel' seems to be likened to a straight and narrow path. Instead of sticking to it, Peter was deviating from it.

What, then, is the truth of the gospel? Every reader of the Epistle to the Galatians should know the answer to this question. It is the good news that we sinners, guilty and under the judgment of God, may be pardoned and accepted by His sheer grace, His free and unmerited favour, on the ground of His Son's death and not for any works or merits of our own. More briefly, the truth of the gospel is the doctrine of justification (which means acceptance before God) by grace alone through faith alone, which he goes on to expound in verses 15–17.

Any deviation from this gospel Paul simply will not tolerate. At the beginning of the Epistle he pronounced a fearful *anathema* on those who distort it (1:8, 9). In Jerusalem he refused to submit to the Judaizers even for a moment, 'that the truth of the gospel might be preserved' (2:5). And now in Antioch, out of the same vehement loyalty to the gospel, he withstands Peter to the face because his behaviour has contradicted it. Paul is determined to defend and uphold the gospel at all costs, even at the expense of publicly humiliating a brother apostle.

But someone may wonder how Peter's withdrawal contradicted the truth of the gospel. Consider Paul's reasoning carefully. Verses

[1] Luther, p. 114.

15, 16: *We ourselves* (that is, Peter and Paul) . . . *know that a man* (any man, whether Jew or Gentile) *is not justified by works of the law but through faith in Jesus Christ.* These words are part of what Paul said to Peter in Antioch. He is reminding him of the gospel which they both knew and which they held in common. On this matter there was no difference of opinion between them. They were agreed that God accepts the sinner through faith in Christ and in the work He finished on the cross. This is the way of salvation for all sinners, Jews and Gentiles alike. There is no distinction between them in the fact of their sin; and there is therefore no distinction between them in the means of their salvation.

Now, if God justifies Jews and Gentiles on the same terms, through simple faith in Christ crucified, and puts no difference between them, who are we to withhold our fellowship from Gentile believers unless they are circumcised? If God does not require this work of the law called circumcision before He accepts them, how dare we impose a condition upon them which He does not impose? If God has accepted them, how can we reject them? If He receives them to *His* fellowship, shall we deny them *ours*? He has reconciled them to Himself; how can we withdraw from those whom God has reconciled? The principle is well stated in Romans 15:9: 'Welcome one another . . ., as Christ has welcomed you.'

Besides, Peter himself had been justified by faith in Jesus. He not only 'knew' the doctrine of justification by faith, but had himself acted on it and 'believed' in Jesus in order to be justified (verse 16). And Peter no longer observed Jewish food regulations. *If you,* Paul says to him, *though a Jew, live like a Gentile and not like a Jew, how can you compel the Gentiles to live like Jews?* (verse 14).

c. What happened as a result

We are not told explicitly in this passage the result of Paul's action, but the perspective of later history tells us. For this incident in Antioch precipitated the future Council in Jerusalem, described in Acts 15. It is possible that Paul was actually on his way up to Jerusalem for the Council while he was writing this Epistle. We know from Acts 15:1, 2 that the dissensions provoked by the Judaizers in Antioch were the immediate cause of the Council. Paul, Barnabas and certain others were appointed by the church to go up to Jerusalem, to the apostles and elders, about this very question. We also know the decision which the Jerusalem Council reached, namely that circumcision was not to be required of Gentile believers. And so, partly as a result of the stand Paul took at Antioch against Peter that day, a great triumph for the gospel was won.

CONCLUSION

What can we learn for today from this clash between Paul and Peter in Antioch? Was it just an undignified, unseemly collision of personalities without any lasting significance? On the contrary, the controversy between Paul and Peter is being re-enacted in contemporary ecclesiastical debate, especially with regard to intercommunion. The scene is different. It is not Syria and Palestine, but other parts of the world, not least England. The participants are also different. They are not first-century apostles, but twentieth-century churchmen. The battleground is different too, for it is not the question of Mosaic circumcision, but of such secondary matters as episcopal confirmation, the mode of baptism or the church's ministry. Yet the fundamental issue at stake is precisely the same, namely on what grounds Christian believers may enjoy table-fellowship with one another, and on what grounds they should separate from one another and excommunicate one another. The answer to these questions is given by the gospel. The gospel is good news of the justification of sinful men by God's grace. It tells us that the sinner's acceptance with God is by faith only, altogether apart from works. This is the truth of the gospel. Once we have grasped it clearly, we are in a position to understand our twofold duty towards it.

a. We must walk straight according to the gospel

It is not enough that we *believe* the gospel (Peter did this, verse 16), nor even that we strive to *preserve* it, as Paul and the Jerusalem apostles did, and the Judaizers did not. We must go further still. We must *apply* it; it is this that Peter failed to do. He knew perfectly well that faith in Jesus was the only condition on which *God* will have fellowship with sinners; but *he* added circumcision as an extra condition on which *he* was prepared to have fellowship with them, thus contradicting the gospel.

Still today various Christian bodies and people repeat Peter's mistake. They refuse to have fellowship with professing Christian believers unless they have been totally immersed in water (no other form of baptism will satisfy them), or unless they have been episcopally confirmed (they insist that only the hands of a bishop in the historic succession will do), or unless their skin has a particular colour, or unless they come out of a certain social drawer (usually the top one), and so on.

All this is a grievous affront to the gospel. Justification is by faith alone; we have no right to add a particular mode of baptism or confirmation or any denominational, racial or social conditions. God does not insist on these things before He accepts us into fellowship; so we must not insist upon them either. What is this ecclesiastical exclusiveness which *we* practise and which *God* does not? Are we more stand-offish than He? The only barrier to communion with God, and therefore with each other, is unbelief, a lack of saving faith in Jesus Christ.

Of course we are not anarchists. There is a place for wholesome church discipline. Every church has the right to make its own rules for its own members. The purpose of such domestic discipline is to ensure, so far as it is possible for human beings to ensure, that those applying for church membership have been justified by faith. But to deny a fellow-Christian (a believing, baptized, communicant member of another church) access to the Lord's table simply because he has not been immersed or confirmed, or is not this or that, is an offence to the God who has justified him, an insult to a brother for whom Christ died and a contradiction of the truth of the gospel. Am I to regard a justified fellow-believer as unclean, that I will not eat with him? We need to hear again the heavenly voice, 'What God has cleansed, you must not call common' (Acts 10:15).

b. We must oppose those who deny the gospel

When the issue between us is trivial, we must be as pliable as possible. But when the truth of the gospel is at stake, we must stand our ground. We thank God for Paul who withstood Peter to his face, for Athanasius who stood against the whole world when

Christendom had embraced the Arian heresy, and for Luther who dared to challenge even the papacy. Where are the men of this calibre today? Many are the vocal pressure groups in the contemporary church. We must not be stampeded into submission to them out of fear. If they oppose the truth of the gospel, we must not hesitate to oppose them.

2:15–21

JUSTIFICATION BY FAITH ALONE

WE ourselves, who are Jews by birth and not Gentile sinners, [16] yet who know that a man is not justified by works of the law but through faith in Jesus Christ, even we have believed in Christ Jesus, in order to be justified by faith in Christ, and not by works of the law, because by works of the law shall no one be justified. [17] But if, in our endeavour to be justified in Christ, we ourselves were found to be sinners, is Christ then an agent of sin? Certainly not! [18] But if I build up again those things which I tore down, then I prove myself a transgressor. [19] For I through the law died to the law, that I might live to God. [20] I have been crucified with Christ; it is no longer I who live, but Christ who lives in me; and the life I now live in the flesh I live by faith in the Son of God, who loved me and gave himself for me. [21] I do not nullify the grace of God; for if justification were through the law, then Christ died to no purpose.

IN these verses an important word occurs for the first time in Galatians. It is central to the message of the Epistle, central to the gospel preached by Paul, and indeed central to Christianity itself. Nobody has understood Christianity who does not understand this word. It is the word 'justified'. The verb comes three times in verse 16 and once in verse 17, while the noun 'justification' occurs in verse 21.

In this paragraph, then, Paul unfolds the great doctrine of justification by faith. It is the good news that sinful men and women may be brought into acceptance with God, not because of their works, but through a simple act of trust in Jesus Christ. Of this doctrine Martin Luther writes: 'This is the truth of the gospel. It is also the principal article of all Christian doctrine, wherein the knowledge of all godliness consisteth. Most necessary it is, therefore, that we should know this article well, teach it unto others, and beat it into their heads continually.'[1] In other places he refers to it

[1] Luther, p. 101.

as the 'chief',[1] the 'chiefest'[2] and 'the most principal and special article of Christian doctrine',[3] for it is this doctrine 'which maketh true Christians indeed'.[4] He adds: 'if the article of justification be once lost, then is all true Christian doctrine lost.'[5]

Similarly, Cranmer wrote in the first Book of Homilies, 'This faith the holy Scripture teacheth: this is the strong rock and foundation of Christian religion: this doctrine all old and ancient authors of Christ's Church do approve: this doctrine advanceth and setteth forth the true glory of Christ, and beateth down the vain glory of man: this whosoever denieth is not to be counted for a true Christian man, nor for a setter forth of Christ's glory, but for an adversary of Christ and His gospel, and for a setter forth of men's vain glory.'[6]

If the doctrine of justification is central to the Christian religion, it is vital that we understand it. What does it mean? 'Justification' is a legal term, borrowed from the law courts. It is the exact opposite of 'condemnation'.[7] 'To condemn' is to declare somebody guilty; 'to justify' is to declare him not guilty, innocent or righteous. In the Bible it refers to God's act of unmerited favour by which He puts a sinner right with Himself, not only pardoning or acquitting him, but accepting him and treating him as righteous.

Many people find Paul's language alien to their vocabulary, and his argument intricate and complex. But is Paul not writing about a universal human need, as pressing today as it was 2,000 years ago? For there are at least two basic things which we know for certain. The first is that God is righteous; the second is that we are not. And if we put these two truths together, they explain our human predicament, of which our conscience and experience have already told us, namely that something is wrong between us and God. Instead of harmony there is friction. We are under the judgment, the just sentence, of God. We are alienated from His fellowship and banished from His presence, for 'what partnership have righteousness and iniquity?' (2 Cor. 6:14).

This being so, the most urgent question facing us is the one which Bildad the Shuhite asked centuries ago, 'How then can man be

[1] Luther, p. 95 [2] Luther, pp. 114, 121. [3] Luther, p. 426.
[4] Luther, p. 143. [5] Luther, p. 26.
[6] Homily entitled 'Of the Salvation of All Mankind' in *Homilies and Canons* (S.P.C.K., 1914), pp. 25, 26.
[7] *Cf.* Dt. 25:1; Pr. 17:15; Rom. 8:33, 34.

righteous before God?' (Jb. 25:4). Or, as Paul would put it, 'How can a condemned sinner be justified?' His answer to these crucial questions is in this paragraph. First, he expounds the doctrine of justification through faith (verses 15, 16). Then he argues it (verses 17–21), dealing with the commonest objection to it and demonstrating the utter impossibility of any alternative.

1. EXPOSITION (verses 15, 16)

His exposition takes the form of a contrast between the Judaizers' doctrine of justification by works of the law and the apostles' doctrine of justification through faith. He repudiates the former and enforces the latter.

a. Justification by works of the law

By 'the law' is meant the sum total of God's commandments, and by 'works of the law' acts done in obedience to it. The Jews supposed they could be justified by this means. So did the Judaizers, who professed to believe in Jesus, but wanted everybody to follow Moses as well. Their position was this: 'The only way to be justified is sheer hard work. You have to toil at it. The "work" you have to do is the "works of the law". That is, you must do everything the law commands and refrain from everything the law forbids.' 'Supremely', the Jews and the Judaizers would go on, 'this means that you must keep the Ten Commandments. You must love and serve the living God, and have no other gods or god-substitutes. You must reverence His name and His day, and honour your parents. You must avoid adultery, murder and theft. You must never bear false witness against your neighbour or covet anything that is his.' But still they have not finished. 'In addition to the moral law, there is the ceremonial law which you must observe. You must be circumcised and join the Jewish church. You must take your religion seriously, searching the Scriptures in private and attending services in public. You must fast and pray and give alms. And if you do all these things, and do not fail in any particular, you will make the grade. God will accept you. You will be justified by "the works of the law".'

Such was the position of the Jew and the Judaizer. Paul describes them as 'seeking to establish their own . . . righteousness' (Rom.

10:3). It has been the religion of the ordinary man both before and since. It is the religion of the man-in-the-street today. Indeed, it is the fundamental principle of every religious and moral system in the world except New Testament Christianity. It is popular because it is flattering. It tells a man that if he will only pull his socks up a bit higher and try a bit harder, he will succeed in winning his own salvation.

But it is all a fearful delusion. It is the biggest lie of the biggest liar the world has ever known, the devil, whom Jesus called 'the father of lies' (Jn. 8:44). Nobody has ever been justified by the works of the law, for the simple reason that nobody has ever perfectly kept the law. The works of the law, a strict adherence to its demands, are beyond us. We may keep some of the law's requirements outwardly, but no man except Jesus Christ has ever kept them all. Indeed, if we look into our hearts, read our thoughts and examine our motives, we find that we have broken all God's laws. For Jesus said that murderous thoughts make us murderers, and adulterous thoughts make us adulterers. No wonder the Scripture tells us: 'by works of the law shall no one be justified' (verse 16, alluding to Ps. 143:2). The astonishing thing is that anybody has ever imagined he could get to God and to heaven that way.

b. Justification through faith

The second alternative Paul calls 'through faith in Jesus Christ'. Jesus Christ came into the world to live and to die. In His life His obedience to the law was perfect. In His death He suffered for our disobedience. On earth He lived the only life of sinless obedience to the law which has ever been lived. On the cross He died for our law-breaking, since the penalty for disobedience to the law was death. All that is required of us to be justified, therefore, is to acknowledge our sin and helplessness, to repent of our years of self-assertion and self-righteousness, and to put our whole trust and confidence in Jesus Christ to save us.

'Faith in Jesus Christ', then, is not intellectual conviction only, but personal commitment. The expression in the middle of verse 16 is (literally) 'we have believed *into* (*eis*) Christ Jesus'. It is an act of committal, not just assenting to the fact that Jesus lived and died, but running to Him for refuge and calling on Him for mercy.

These, then, are theoretically the two alternative means of justification: 'by works of the law' and 'through faith in Jesus Christ'. And three times over Paul tells us that God's way is the second, not the first. His emphatic triple statement in verse 16 is intended to leave us in no doubt about this matter, and (as Luther often said) to 'beat it into our heads'. Not that the repetition is exact and monotonous, however, for there is an ascending scale of emphasis—first general, then personal, and finally universal.

The first statement is general (verse 16a). We 'know that *a man* is not justified by works of the law but through faith in Jesus Christ'. Paul has nobody specially in mind here; he is deliberately vague. Just 'a man', any man, any woman. Further, he says, 'We know'. He does not offer a tentative opinion, but a dogmatic assertion. He has spent much of the first two chapters of the Epistle defending his apostolic authority; now he lends the full weight of his authority to this statement. He has dared to claim that his gospel was 'not man's gospel' (1:11). This being the case, his exposition of the gospel in verse 16 is not man's, but God's. Moreover, the plural '*we* know' means in the context that the apostles Peter and Paul both know it, that they are united in their conviction about the nature of the gospel.

The second statement is personal (verse 16b). Not only do 'we ourselves . . . know', but 'even we have believed in Christ Jesus, in order to be justified by faith in Christ'. That is, our certainty about the gospel is more than intellectual; we have proved it personally in our own experience. This is an important addition. It shows that Paul is propounding a doctrine which he has himself put to the test. 'We know it,' he says, 'and we have ourselves believed in Christ, in order to prove it.'

The third statement is universal (verse 16c). The theological principle and the personal experience are now confirmed by Scripture. The apostle quotes the categorical statement of Psalm 143:2 (as he does again in Rom. 3:20): 'because by works of the law shall no one be justified.' The Greek expression is even more striking than the English. It refers to 'all flesh', mankind without exception. Whatever our religious upbringing, educational background, social status or racial origin, the way of salvation is the same. None can be justified by works of the law; all flesh must be justified through faith in Christ.

It would be hard to find a more forceful statement of the doctrine of justification than this. It is insisted upon by the two leading apostles ('we know'), confirmed from their own experience ('we have believed'), and endorsed by the sacred Scriptures of the Old Testament ('by works of the law shall no one be justified'). With this threefold guarantee we should accept the biblical doctrine of justification and not let our natural self-righteousness keep us from faith in Christ.

2. ARGUMENT (verses 17–21)

Plain and pungent as Paul's exposition is, it was challenged in his day, and it is still being challenged today. So in these verses he turns from exposition to argument. He tells us both the argument which his critics used to try to overthrow his doctrine, and the argument which he used to overthrow their doctrine and to establish his. We hear them arguing with one another, as it were.

a. The critics' argument against Paul (verses 17–20)

Verses 17, 18: *But if, in our endeavour to be justified in Christ, we ourselves were found to be sinners, is Christ then an agent of sin? Certainly not! But if I build up again those things which I tore down, then I prove myself a transgressor.* These verses are not easy, and have been differently understood. Of the two main interpretations, I have chosen that which seems the more consistent with Paul's writing elsewhere, and in particular with the parallel teaching in the Epistle to the Romans.

Paul's critics argued like this: 'Your doctrine of justification through faith in Christ only, apart from the works of the law, is a highly dangerous doctrine. It fatally weakens a man's sense of moral responsibility. If he can be accepted through trusting in Christ, without any necessity to do good works, you are actually encouraging him to break the law, which is the vile heresy of "antinomianism".' People still argue like this today: 'If God justifies bad people, what is the point of being good? Can't we do as we like and live as we please?'

Paul's first response to his critics is to deny their suggestion with hot indignation: 'God forbid' he says (verse 17, AV). He specially denies the added allegation that he was guilty of making Christ the agent or author of men's sins. On the contrary, he goes on, 'I make myself a transgressor' (verse 18, AV). In other words, 'if after my justification I am still a sinner, it is my fault and not Christ's. I have only myself to blame; no-one can blame Christ.'

Paul now proceeds to refute his critics' argument. Their charge that justification by faith encouraged a continuance in sin was ludicrous. They grossly misunderstood the gospel of justification. Justification is not a legal fiction, in which a man's status is changed, while his character is left untouched. Verse 17: We are 'justified *in Christ*'. That is, our justification takes place when we are united to Christ by faith. And someone who is united to Christ is never the same person again. Instead, he is changed. It is not just his standing before God which has changed; it is he himself—radically, permanently changed. To talk of his going back to the old life, and even sinning as he pleases, is frankly impossible. He has become a new creation and begun a new life.

This amazing change, which comes over somebody who is justified in Christ, Paul now unfolds. He describes it in terms of a death and a resurrection. Twice in verses 19 and 20 he speaks of this dying and this rising to life again. Both take place through union with Christ. It is *Christ's* death and resurrection in which we share. Verse 19: *For I through the law died to the law* (the law's demand of death was satisfied in the death of Christ), *that I might live to God.* Verse 20: *I have been crucified with Christ* (that is, being united to Christ in His sin-bearing death, my sinful past has been blotted out)*; it is no longer I who live, but Christ who lives in me; and the life I now live in the flesh I live by faith in the Son of God, who loved me and gave himself for me.*

Perhaps now it is becoming clearer why a Christian who is 'justified in Christ' is not free to sin. In Christ 'old things are passed away' and 'all things are become new' (2 Cor. 5:17, AV). This is because the death and resurrection of Christ are not only historical events (He 'gave himself' and now 'lives'), but events in which through faith-union with Him His people have come to share ('I have been crucified with Christ' and now 'I live'). Once we have been united to Christ in His death, our old life is finished; it is ridiculous to suggest that we could ever go back to it. Besides, we have risen to a new life. In one sense, we live this new life through faith in Christ. In another sense, it is not we who live it at all, but

Christ who lives it in us. And, living in us, He gives us new desires for holiness, for God, for heaven. It is not that we cannot sin again; we can. But we do not want to. The whole tenor of our life has changed. Everything is different now, because we ourselves are different. See how daringly personal Paul makes it: Christ 'gave himself for *me*'. 'Christ . . . lives in *me*.' No Christian who has grasped these truths could ever seriously contemplate reverting to the old life.

b. Paul's argument against his critics (verse 21)

We have seen how Paul counters his critics' attempt to overthrow his doctrine; we must now consider how he sets about overthrowing theirs. Verse 21: *I do not* (NEB 'will not') *nullify the grace of God; for if justification were through the law, then Christ died to no purpose.* We must try to feel the force of this argument. The two foundation planks of the Christian religion are the grace of God and the death of Christ. The Christian gospel is the gospel of the grace of God. The Christian faith is the faith of Christ crucified. So if anybody insists that justification is by works, and that he can earn his salvation by his own efforts, he is undermining the foundations of the Christian religion. He is nullifying the grace of God (because if salvation is by works, it is not by grace) and he is making Christ's death superfluous (because if salvation is our own work, then Christ's work was unnecessary).

Yet there are large numbers of people who, like the Judaizers, are making these very mistakes. They are seeking to commend themselves to God by their own works. They think it noble to try to win their way to God and to heaven. But it is not noble; it is dreadfully ignoble. For, in effect, it is to deny both the nature of God and the mission of Christ. It is to refuse to let God be gracious. It is to tell Christ that He need not have bothered to die. For both the grace of God and the death of Christ become redundant, if we are masters of our own destiny and can save ourselves.

CONCLUSION

Four Christian truths seem to stand out from this paragraph.

First, man's greatest need is justification, or acceptance with God.

In comparison with this, all other human needs pale into insignificance. How can we be put right with God, so that we spend time and eternity in His favour and service?

Secondly, justification is not by works of the law, but through faith in Christ. Luther expresses it succinctly: 'I must hearken to the Gospel, which teacheth me, not what I ought to do (for that is the proper office of the Law), but what Jesus Christ the Son of God hath done for me: to wit, that he suffered and died to deliver me from sin and death.'[1]

Thirdly, not to trust in Jesus Christ, because of self-trust, is an insult both to the grace of God and to the cross of Christ, for it declares both to be unnecessary.

Fourthly, to trust in Jesus Christ, and thus to become united to Him, is to begin an altogether new life. If we are 'in Christ', we are more than justified; we find that we have actually died and risen with Him. So we are able to say with Paul: *I have been crucified with Christ; it is no longer I who live, but Christ who lives in me; and the life I now live in the flesh I live by faith in the Son of God, who loved me and gave himself for me* (verse 20).

[1] Luther, p. 101.

3:1–9

THE FOLLY OF THE GALATIANS

O FOOLISH *Galatians! Who has bewitched you, before whose eyes Jesus Christ was publicly portrayed as crucified?* [2] *Let me ask you only this: Did you receive the Spirit by works of the law, or by hearing with faith?* [3] *Are you so foolish? Having begun with the Spirit, are you now ending with the flesh?* [4] *Did you experience so many things in vain?—if it really is in vain.* [5] *Does he who supplies the Spirit to you and works miracles among you do so by works of the law, or by hearing with faith?*

[6] *Thus Abraham 'believed God, and it was reckoned to him as righteousness.'* [7] *So you see that it is men of faith who are the sons of Abraham.* [8] *And the scripture, foreseeing that God would justify the Gentiles by faith, preached the gospel beforehand to Abraham, saying, 'In you shall all the nations be blessed.'* [9] *So then, those who are men of faith are blessed with Abraham who had faith.*

THROUGHOUT most of chapters 1 and 2 Paul has been stoutly defending the divine origin of his apostolic mission and message. They had been derived from God, he insists, and were independent of men.

Now he comes back to the Galatians, and to their unfaithfulness to the gospel as a result of the corrupting influence of the false teachers. Verse 1: 'O foolish Galatians!' Verse 3: 'Are you so foolish?' Or, as J. B. Phillips puts it, 'O you dear idiots of Galatia . . . surely you can't be so idiotic . . . ?' The Galatians' turning away from the gospel, therefore, was not only a kind of spiritual treason (1:6), but also an act of folly. Indeed, so stupid was it that Paul wonders if some sorcerer 'has bewitched' them or 'has been casting a spell' (JBP) over them. His question is partly rhetorical, because he knows only too well about the activities of the false teachers. But perhaps he uses the singular ('who . . . ?') because behind these false teachers he detects the activity of the devil himself, the deceiving spirit, whom the Lord Jesus called 'a liar and the father of lies' (Jn. 8:44).

Much of our Christian stupidity in grasping and applying the gospel may be due to the spells which he casts.

What have the Galatians done, which leads Paul to complain of their senselessness and to ask if they have been bewitched? They have yielded to the teaching of the Judaizers. Having embraced the truth at the beginning (that sinners are justified by grace, in Christ, through faith), they have now adopted the view that circumcision and the works of the law are also necessary for justification.

The essence of Paul's argument is that their new position is a contradiction of the gospel. The reason for his astonishment at their folly is that before their very eyes Jesus Christ has been 'publicly portrayed as crucified'. It is not just that Christ was publicly portrayed before their eyes, but that He was portrayed before them *as crucified* (an emphatic participle at the end of the sentence). It is possible that Paul is making a further allusion to their having been bewitched. He seems to be asking how some sorcerer could have put them under the spell of an evil eye, when before their very eyes Christ has been portrayed as crucified.

This, then, is the gospel. It is not a general instruction about the Jesus of history, but a specific proclamation of Jesus Christ as crucified (*cf.* 1 Cor. 1:23; 2:2). The force of the perfect tense of the participle (*estaurōmenos*) is that Christ's work was completed on the cross, and that the benefits of His crucifixion are for ever fresh, valid and available. Sinners may be justified before God and by God, not because of any works of their own, but because of the atoning work of Christ; not because of anything that they have done or could do, but because of what Christ did once, when He died. The gospel is not good advice to men, but good news about Christ; not an invitation to us to do anything, but a declaration of what God has done; not a demand, but an offer.

And if the Galatians had grasped the gospel of Christ crucified, that on the cross Christ did everything necessary for our salvation, they would have realized that the only thing required of them was to receive the good news by faith. To add good works to the work of Christ was an offence to His finished work, as we saw in 2:21.

Paul now exposes the senselessness of the Galatians. They should have resisted the spell of whoever was bewitching them. They knew perfectly well that the gospel is received by faith alone, since their own experience (verses 2–5) and the plain teaching of Scripture (verses 6–9) had told them so.

1. THE ARGUMENT FROM THEIR OWN EXPERIENCE (verses 2–5)

Verse 2: *Let me ask you only this: Did you receive the Spirit by works of the law, or by hearing with faith?* Verse 4: *Did you experience so many things in vain?* Paul assumes that they have all received the Spirit. His question is not whether they have received Him, but whether they received Him by works or by faith (verse 2). He assumes also that this is how their Christian life began (verse 3: *having begun with the Spirit*). What he is asking concerns *how* they received the Spirit and so began the Christian life. What part did they play in the process?

It is important to be clear about the possible alternatives, which the apostle terms 'by works of the law' (*i.e.* by obeying the law's demands) and 'by hearing with faith' (*i.e.* 'believing the gospel message', NEB). The contrast, already adumbrated in 2:16, is between the law and the gospel. As Luther writes: 'Whoso . . . can rightly judge between the law and the Gospel, let him thank God, and know that he is a right divine.'[1] This is the difference between them: the law says 'Do this'; the gospel says 'Christ has done it all'. The law requires works of human achievement; the gospel requires faith in Christ's achievement. The law makes demands and bids us obey; the gospel brings promises and bids us believe. So the law and the gospel are contrary to one another. They are not two aspects of the same thing, or interpretations of the same Christianity. At least in the sphere of justification, as Luther says, 'the establishing of the law is the abolishing of the Gospel'.[2]

In verse 5 Paul uses the same argument in a second way—not now from the point of view of *their* receiving the Spirit, but from the point of view of *God* giving the Spirit: *Does he* (that is, God) *who supplies the Spirit to you and works miracles among you do so by works of the law, or by hearing with faith?* The verbs 'supplies' and 'works' do not necessarily refer to a continuous activity of God. It seems more probable that they are timeless, referring still to Paul's visit when they received the Spirit, but that now he is speaking of their experience from God's point of view. When Paul visited Galatia,

[1] Luther, p. 122. [2] *Ibid.*

God gave them the Spirit and worked miracles through him ('the signs of a true apostle', 2 Cor. 12:12). The question is the same: '*How* did God do these works among them?' And the answer is the same: Not 'by works of the law', but 'through hearing with faith'. God gave them the Spirit (verse 5) and they received the Spirit (verse 2), not because they obeyed the law, but because they believed the gospel.

This, then, was a fact of their experience. Paul had come to Galatia and preached the gospel to them. He had publicly portrayed before their eyes Jesus Christ as crucified. They had heard the gospel and with the eye of faith had seen Christ displayed upon His cross. They had believed the gospel. They had trusted in the Christ exhibited in the gospel. So they had received the Spirit. They had neither submitted to circumcision, nor obeyed the law, nor even tried to. All they had done was to hear the gospel and believe, and the Spirit had been given to them. These being the facts of their experience, Paul argues, it is ludicrous that, 'having begun with the Spirit', they should now expect to complete 'with the flesh'. This is another way of saying that, having begun with the gospel, they must not go back to the law, imagining that the law was needed to supplement the gospel. To do so would be not 'improvement' but 'degeneracy'.[1]

2. THE ARGUMENT FROM OLD TESTAMENT SCRIPTURE (verses 6–9)

Verse 6: *Thus Abraham 'believed God, and it was reckoned to him as righteousness.'* Paul's allusion to Abraham was a master-stroke. His Judaizing opponents looked to Moses as their teacher. So Paul went centuries further back to Abraham himself. His quotation is from Genesis 15:6. Let me remind you of the circumstances. Abraham was an old man and childless, but God had promised him a son, and indeed a seed or posterity. One day He took Abraham out of his tent, told him to look up at the sky and count the stars, and then said to him: 'So shall your descendants be.' Abraham believed God's promise, 'and it was reckoned to him as righteousness'.

Consider carefully what happened. First, God made Abraham a promise. Indeed, the promise of descendants was 'placarded' before

[1] Brown, p. 111.

Abraham's eyes, much as the promise of forgiveness through Christ crucified was 'placarded' before the eyes of the Galatians. Secondly, Abraham believed God. Despite the inherent improbability of the promise, from the human point of view, Abraham cast himself on the faithfulness of God. Thirdly, Abraham's faith was reckoned as righteousness. That is, he was himself accepted as righteous, by faith. He was not justified because he had done anything to deserve it, or because he had been circumcised, or because he had kept the law (for neither circumcision nor the law had yet been given), but simply because he believed God.

With this promise of God to Abraham Paul now links another and earlier promise. Verses 7–9: *So you see that it is men of faith who are the sons of Abraham. And the scripture, foreseeing that God would justify the Gentiles by faith, preached the gospel beforehand to Abraham, saying, 'In you shall all the nations be blessed.' So then, those who are men of faith are blessed with Abraham who had faith.* Here Paul is quoting from Genesis 12:3 (*cf.* Gn. 22:17, 18; Acts 3:25). We must examine what this blessing was, and how all nations would come to inherit it. The blessing is justification, the greatest of all blessings, for the verbs 'to justify' and 'to bless' are used as equivalents in verse 8. And the means by which the blessing would be inherited is faith ('God would justify the Gentiles by faith'), which was the only way in which *Gentiles* could inherit Abraham's blessing since Abraham was the father of the Jewish race. Perhaps the Judaizers were telling the Galatian converts that they should become the sons of Abraham by circumcision. So Paul counters by saying that the Galatians were *already* the sons of Abraham, not by circumcision but by faith.

Both verses 7 and 9 affirm that the true children of Abraham (who inherit the blessing promised to his seed) are not his posterity by *physical* descent, the Jews, but his *spiritual* progeny, men and women who share his faith, namely Christian believers.

All this, the apostle says, the Galatians should have known. They should never have been so foolish. They should never have fallen under the spell of these false teachers. Indeed, they would not have done so, if they had kept Christ crucified before their eyes. They should have realized at once that the Judaizers were contradicting the gospel of justification by faith alone. They should have known it, as we have seen, from their own experience and from the Scriptures of the Old Testament.

We too should learn to test every theory and teaching of men by the gospel of Christ crucified, especially as it is known to us from Scripture and from experience.

CONCLUSION

a. What the gospel is

The gospel is Christ crucified, His finished work on the cross. And to preach the gospel is publicly to portray Christ as crucified. The gospel is not good news primarily of a baby in a manger, a young man at a carpenter's bench, a preacher in the fields of Galilee, or even an empty tomb. The gospel concerns Christ upon His cross. Only when Christ is 'openly displayed upon his cross' (NEB) is the gospel preached. This verb *prographein* means to 'show forth or portray publicly, proclaim or placard in public' (Arndt-Gingrich). It was used of edicts, laws and public notices, which were put up in some public place to be read, and also of pictures and portraits.

This means that in preaching the gospel we are to refer to an event (Christ's death on a cross), to expound a doctrine (the perfect participle 'crucified' indicating the abiding effects of Christ's finished work), and to do so publicly, boldly, vividly, so that people see it as if they witnessed it with their own eyes. This is what some writers have called the 'existential' element in preaching. We do more than describe the cross as a first-century event. We actually portray Christ crucified before the eyes of our contemporaries, so that they are confronted by Christ crucified *today* and realize that they may receive from the cross the salvation of God *today*.

b. What the gospel offers

On the ground of Christ's cross, the gospel offers a great blessing. Verse 8: 'In you shall all the nations be *blessed*.' What is this? It is a double blessing. The first part is justification (verse 8) and the second the gift of the Spirit (verses 2–5). It is with these two gifts that God blesses all who are in Christ. He both justifies us, accepting us as righteous in His sight, and puts His Spirit within us. What is more, He never bestows one gift without the other. Everybody who receives the Spirit is justified, and everybody who is justified receives the Spirit. It is important to notice this double initial blessing, since various people nowadays are teaching instead a doctrine of salvation in two stages, that we are justified at the beginning and receive the Spirit only at a later stage.

c. What the gospel requires

The gospel offers blessings; what must we do to receive them? The proper answer is 'nothing'! We do not have to *do* anything. We have only to *believe*. Our response is not 'the works of the law' but 'hearing with faith', that is, not obeying the law, but believing the gospel. For obeying is to attempt to do the work of salvation ourselves, whereas believing is to let Christ be our Saviour and to rest in His finished work. So Paul emphasizes both that we receive the Spirit by faith (verses 2 and 5) and that we are justified by faith (verse 8). Indeed, the noun 'faith' and the verb 'to believe' occur seven times in this brief paragraph (verses 1–9).

Such is the true gospel, the gospel of the Old and New Testaments, the gospel which God Himself began to preach to Abraham (verse 8) and which the apostle Paul continued to preach in his day. It is the setting forth before men's eyes of Jesus Christ as crucified. It offers on this basis both justification and the gift of the Spirit. And its only demand is faith.

3:10–14
THE ALTERNATIVE OF FAITH AND WORKS

FOR *all who rely on works of the law are under a curse; for it is written, 'Cursed be every one who does not abide by all things written in the book of the law, and do them.'* [11] *Now it is evident that no man is justified before God by the law; for 'He who through faith is righteous shall live';* [12] *but the law does not rest on faith, for 'He who does them shall live by them.'* [13] *Christ redeemed us from the curse of the law, having become a curse for us—for it is written, 'Cursed be every one who hangs on a tree'—*[14] *that in Christ Jesus the blessing of Abraham might come upon the Gentiles, that we might receive the promise of the Spirit through faith.*

THESE verses may seem difficult in both concept and vocabulary, yet they are fundamental to an understanding of biblical Christianity. For they concern the central issue of religion, which is how to come into a right relationship with God. This is described in two ways. First, it is called being 'justified before God' (verse 11). To be 'justified before God' is the exact opposite of being condemned by Him. It is to be declared righteous, to be accepted, to stand in His favour and under His smile. Clearly, this is a matter of the first importance. Human beings have an instinctive desire to be in favour with their fellows, friend with friend, children with their parents, an employee with his boss. Similarly, although we are by nature in revolt against God, we still long to be put right with Him.

The second description of a person who finds God is this: 'he . . . shall live' (verses 11, 12) or 'he shall gain life' (NEB). The life referred to here is, of course, not physical and biological, but spiritual and eternal, not the life of this age, but the life of the age to come. The simplest definition of eternal life in the Bible comes from the lips of our Lord Jesus Christ Himself: 'this is eternal life, that they know thee the only true God, and Jesus Christ whom thou hast sent' (Jn. 17:3).

So 'justification' means to be in favour with God; 'eternal life' means to be in fellowship with God. And the two are closely, indeed indissolubly, related. We cannot be in fellowship with God until we are in favour with Him; and once we are in favour with Him, fellowship with Him is granted to us too.

The question before us now is: *how* can a man enter the favour and the fellowship of God? In Paul's terms, how can a sinner be 'justified' and receive 'eternal life'? These verses give us the answer, plainly and unequivocally. We shall begin by considering the two alternative answers which men have given to our question. Then we shall see how one is false and the other true.

1. THE TWO ALTERNATIVES (verses 11, 12)

The apostle quotes twice from the Old Testament: *he who through faith is righteous shall live* (verse 11) and *he who does them* (that is, the requirements of the law) *shall live by them* (verse 12). We must look carefully at these two statements. Both come from Old Testament Scripture, the first from the prophets (Hab. 2:4), the second from the law (Lv. 18:5). Both are therefore the word of the living God. Both say of a certain man that 'he shall live'. In other words, both promise him eternal life.

Despite these common features, however, the two statements describe a different road to life. The first promises life to the believer, the second to the doer. The first makes faith the way of salvation, the second, works. The first says that only God can justify (because the whole function of faith is to trust God to do the work), the second implies that we can manage by ourselves.

These are the two alternatives. Which is true? Is a man justified by faith or by works? Do we receive eternal life by believing or by doing? Is salvation entirely and only by the free grace of God in Jesus Christ or do we have some hand in it ourselves? And why does the Bible seem here to confuse the issue and teach both, when they appear to us to be contradictory?

2. THE ALTERNATIVE OF WORKS (verse 10)

All who rely on works of the law are under a curse; for it is written, 'Cursed be every one who does not abide by all things written in the book of the law, and do them.' This is yet another Old Testament quotation (Dt. 27:26), for the apostle is at pains to show, as he was later to say to King Agrippa, that he was teaching 'nothing but what the prophets and Moses said . . .' (Acts 26:22). In this verse from Deuteronomy a solemn curse is pronounced on every one who fails to keep all the commandments of the law. It is true that the word 'all' seems to have been imported into Deuteronomy 27:26 from the following verse (28:1), but it does not change the sense.

To our modern and sensitive ears these words sound crude and even harsh. We like to think of a God who blesses rather than of a God who curses. Some people have tried to escape the dilemma by pointing out that Paul writes not of the curse of God, but of 'the curse of the law' (verse 13). It is very doubtful, however, if the biblical authors would have recognized this distinction. The law can never be isolated from God, for the law is God's law, the expression of His moral nature and will. What the law says, God says; what the law blesses, God blesses; and what the law curses, God curses.

Indeed, there is no need to be embarrassed by these outspoken words. They express what Scripture everywhere tells us about God in relation to sin, namely that no man can sin with impunity, for God is not a sentimental old Father Christmas, but the righteous Judge of men. Disobedience always brings us under the curse of God, and exposes us to the awful penalties of His judgment, to 'curse' meaning not to 'denounce' but actually to 'reject'. So if the blessing of God brings justification and life, the curse of God brings condemnation and death.

This is the position of every human being who has ever lived, except Jesus Christ. Paul assumes the universality of sin here; he argues it in the early chapters of the Epistle to the Romans. It includes righteous and respectable people, who think that they are excluded. Dr. Alan Cole comments[1] that it was the *am haaretz*, the common people without the law, whom the Jews regarded as being under God's curse. But the apostle here shocks the Judaizers by asserting that the people who are under the curse are not just the ignorant, lawless Gentiles, as they imagine, but the Jews themselves as well. As he writes in Romans: 'there is no distinction (*i.e.* between Jew and Gentile); since all have sinned and fall short of the glory of God' (Rom. 3:22, 23).

[1] Cole, p. 95.

We know this in our own experience. John defines sin as 'lawlessness' (1 Jn. 3:4), a disregard for the laws of God. And all of us are lawless, for we have neither loved God with all our being, nor our neighbour as ourselves. Further, having broken the laws of God, we have brought ourselves under the curse of the law, which is the curse of God. This is true of all men, not only the irreligious and the immoral, but Jews descended from Abraham, who were circumcised and in the covenant of God, yes and (to apply it to ourselves today) even baptized churchmen too. 'Cursed are all who do not persevere in doing everything that is written in the Book of the Law' (verse 10, NEB).

So this is why no man can be justified before God by works of the law. It is quite true, as an axiom, that 'he who does them shall live by them' (verse 12). But nobody has ever done them; therefore nobody can live by them. Because everybody has failed to keep the law (except Jesus), Paul has to write that 'all who rely on works of the law are under a curse' (verse 10). The dreadful function of the law is to condemn, not to justify. We may strive and struggle to keep the law, and to do good works in the community or the church, but none of these things can deliver us from the curse of the law which rests upon the lawbreaker.

So this first supposed road to God leads to a dead end. There is neither justification nor life that way, but only darkness and death. We cannot help concluding, as Paul does: *Now it is evident that no man is justified before God by the law* (verse 11a).

3. THE ALTERNATIVE OF FAITH (verses 13, 14)

This second alternative introduces Jesus Christ. It tells us that Jesus Christ has done for us on the cross what we could not do for ourselves. The only way to escape the curse is not by our work, but by His. He has redeemed us, ransomed us, set us free from the awful condition of bondage to which the curse of the law had brought us. Verse 13: *Christ redeemed us from the curse of the law, having become a curse for us.* These are astonishing words. As Bishop Blunt put it: 'the language here is startling, almost shocking. We should not have dared to use it. Yet Paul means every word of it.'[1]

[1] *The Epistle of Paul to the Galatians*, by A. W. F. Blunt (*The Clarendon Bible*, Oxford, 1925), pp. 96, 97.

In its context, in which it must be read, the phrase can mean only one thing, for the 'curse' of verses 10 and 13 is evidently the same curse. The 'curse of the law' from which Christ redeemed us must be the curse resting upon us for our disobedience (verse 10). And He redeemed us from it by 'becoming a curse' Himself. The curse was transferred from us to Him. He took it voluntarily upon Himself, in order to deliver us from it. It is this 'becoming a curse for us' which explains the awful cry of dereliction, of God-forsakenness, which He uttered from the cross.

Paul now adds a scriptural confirmation of what he has just said about the cross. He quotes Deuteronomy 21:23: *for it is written, 'Cursed be every one who hangs on a tree'* (verse 13b). Every criminal sentenced to death under the Mosaic legislation and executed, usually by stoning, was then fixed to a stake or 'hanged on a tree' as a symbol of his divine rejection. Dr. Cole says the quotation means 'not . . . that a man is cursed by God because he is hanged, but that death by hanging was the outward sign in Israel of a man who was thus cursed'.[1] The fact that the Romans executed by crucifixion rather than hanging makes no difference. To be nailed to a cross was equivalent to being hanged on a tree. So Christ crucified was described as having been 'hanged on a tree' (*e.g.* Acts 5:30; 1 Pet. 2:24), and was recognized as having died under the divine curse. No wonder the Jews at first could not believe that Jesus was the Christ. How could Christ, the anointed of God, instead of reigning on a throne, hang on a tree? It was incredible to them. Perhaps, as Bishop Stephen Neill suggests,[2] when Christ crucified was preached, Jews would sometimes shout back 'Jesus is accursed!', which is the dreadful ejaculation mentioned in 1 Corinthians 12:3.

The fact that Jesus died hanging on a tree remained for Jews an insurmountable obstacle to faith, until they saw that the curse He bore was for *them*. He did not die for His own sins; He became a curse 'for us'.

Does this mean that everybody has been redeemed from the law's curse through the sin-bearing, curse-bearing cross of Christ? Indeed not, for verse 13 must not be read without verse 14, where it is written that Christ became a curse for us, *that in Christ Jesus the blessing of Abraham might come upon the Gentiles, that we might receive*

[1] Cole, p. 99. [2] Neill, pp. 41, 42.

the promise of the Spirit through faith. It was *in Christ* that God acted for our salvation, and so we must be *in Christ* to receive it. We are not saved by a distant Christ, who died hundreds of years ago and lives millions of miles away, but by an existential Christ, who, having died and risen again, is now our contemporary. As a result we can be 'in Him', personally and vitally united to Him today.

But how? Granted that He bore our curse, and that we must be 'in Him' to be redeemed from it, how do we become united to Him? The answer is 'through faith'. Paul has already quoted Habakkuk: 'he who *through faith* is righteous shall live' (verse 11). Now he says it himself: 'We . . . receive the promise of the Spirit *through faith*' (verse 14).

Faith is laying hold of Jesus Christ personally. There is no merit in it. It is not another 'work'. Its value is not in itself, but entirely in its object, Jesus Christ. As Luther put it, 'faith . . . apprehendeth nothing else but that precious jewel Christ Jesus.'[1] Christ is the Bread of life; faith feeds upon Him. Christ was lifted up on the cross; faith gazes at Him there.

CONCLUSION

The apostle sets the alternatives before us in the starkest contrast. He tells us of two destinies, and of two possible roads by which to reach them. He speaks like a kind of New Testament Moses, for Moses said: 'I have set before you life and death, blessing and curse' (Dt. 30:19).

a. The two destinies

Like Moses, Paul calls the two destinies of man 'blessing' and 'curse'. It is very striking to see them contrasted in verses 13 and 14, where it is written that Christ became a curse for us, that we might inherit a blessing. So far we have concentrated on the curse; what is the blessing? It is termed 'the blessing of Abraham' (verse 14), partly because it is the blessing which Abraham himself received when he believed, and partly because God said to him: 'I will bless you . . .; and in you all the families of the earth will be blessed' (Gn. 12:2, 3, RSV mg.). As it is unfolded in these verses, the promised

[1] Luther, p. 100.

blessing includes justification (being put into favour with God), eternal life (being received into fellowship with God) and 'the promise of the Spirit' (being regenerated and indwelt by Him). This is the priceless threefold 'blessing' of the Christian believer.

b. The two roads

By what roads do we attain to the 'curse' and the 'blessing'? The first road is called 'the law'; those who travel by it are those 'who rely on works of the law' (verse 10); they are 'under a curse'. The second road is called 'faith'; those who travel by it are 'men of faith' (verses 7, 9); they inherit the 'blessing'. The first group trust in their own works, the second in the finished work of Christ.

The challenge of this passage is straightforward. We must renounce the proud folly of supposing that we can establish our own righteousness or make ourselves acceptable to God. Instead we must come humbly to the cross, where Christ bore our curse, and cast ourselves entirely upon His mercy. And then, by God's sheer grace, because we are in Christ Jesus by faith, we shall receive justification, eternal life and the indwelling Spirit. The 'blessing of Abraham' will be ours.

3:15–22

ABRAHAM, MOSES AND CHRIST

TO give a human example, brethren: no one annuls even a man's will, or adds to it, once it has been ratified. [16] *Now the promises were made to Abraham and to his offspring. It does not say, 'And to offsprings,' referring to many; but, referring to one, 'And to your offspring,' which is Christ.* [17] *This is what I mean: the law, which came four hundred and thirty years afterward, does not annul a covenant previously ratified by God, so as to make the promise void.* [18] *For if the inheritance is by the law, it is no longer by promise; but God gave it to Abraham by a promise.*

[19] *Why then the law? It was added because of transgressions, till the offspring should come to whom the promise had been made; and it was ordained by angels through an intermediary.* [20] *Now an intermediary implies more than one; but God is one.*

[21] *Is the law then against the promises of God? Certainly not; for if a law had been given which could make alive, then righteousness would indeed be by the law.* [22] *But the scripture consigned all things to sin, that what was promised to faith in Jesus Christ might be given to those who believe.*

THE apostle Paul is still expounding 'the truth of the gospel', namely that salvation is a free gift of God, received through faith in Christ crucified, irrespective of any human merit. He is emphasizing this, because the Judaizers could not accept the principle of *sola fides*, 'faith alone'. They insisted that men must contribute something to their salvation. So they were adding to faith in Jesus 'the works of the law' as another essential ground of acceptance with God.

The way Paul hammers home God's plan of free salvation is from the Old Testament. In order to understand his argument, and to feel its force, we need to grasp both the history and the theology which lie behind its reasoning.

a. The history

Paul takes us back to about 2000 BC, to Abraham, and then on to Moses who lived some centuries later. Moses is not named here, but he is without doubt the 'intermediary' (verse 19), through whom the law was given.

Let me remind you of this part of the Old Testament story. God called Abraham from Ur of the Chaldees. He promised that He would give him an innumerable 'seed' (or posterity), that He would bestow on him and on his seed a land, and that in his seed all the families of the earth would be blessed. These great promises of God to Abraham were confirmed to Abraham's son Isaac, and then to Isaac's son Jacob. But Jacob died outside the promised land, in Egyptian exile, to which a famine in Canaan had driven him. Jacob's twelve sons died in exile too. Centuries passed. A period of 430 years is mentioned (verse 17), which refers not to the time between Abraham and Moses, but to the duration of the bondage in Egypt (Ex. 12:40; *cf.* Gn. 15:13; Acts 7:6). Finally, centuries after Abraham, God raised up Moses, and through him both delivered the Israelites from their slavery and gave them the law at Mount Sinai. This, briefly, is the history which links Moses to Abraham.

b. The theology

God's dealings with Abraham and Moses were based on two different principles. To Abraham He gave a promise ('I will show you a land . . . I will bless you . . .', Gn. 12:1, 2). But to Moses He gave the law, summarized in the Ten Commandments. 'These two things (as I do often repeat),' comments Luther,[1] 'to wit, the law and the promise, must be diligently distinguished. For in time, in place, and in person, and generally in all other circumstances, they are separate as far asunder as heaven and earth. . . .' Again,[2] 'unless the Gospel be plainly discerned from the law, the true Christian doctrine cannot be kept sound and uncorrupt.' What is the difference between them? In the promise to Abraham God said, 'I will . . . I will . . . I will . . .'. But in the law of Moses God said, 'Thou shalt . . . thou shalt not . . .'. The promise sets forth a religion of God—

[1] Luther, p. 291. [2] Luther, p. 302.

God's plan, God's grace, God's initiative. But the law sets forth a religion of man—man's duty, man's works, man's responsibility. The promise (standing for the grace of God) had only to be believed. But the law (standing for the works of men) had to be obeyed. God's dealings with Abraham were in the category of 'promise', 'grace' and 'faith'. But God's dealings with Moses were in the category of 'law', 'commandments' and 'works'.

The conclusion to which Paul is leading is that the Christian religion is the religion of Abraham and not Moses, of promise and not law; and that Christians are enjoying today the promise which God made to Abraham centuries ago. But in this passage, having contrasted these two kinds of religion, he shows the relation between them. After all, the God who gave the promise to Abraham and the God who gave the law to Moses are the same God! Some commentators think that this is the meaning of the enigmatic phrase 'God is one' (verse 20), namely that the God of Abraham and the God of Moses are one and the same God. We cannot set Abraham and Moses, the promise and the law, against each other, accepting the one and rejecting the other, *tout simple*. If God is the author of both, He must have had some purpose for both. What, then, is the relation between them?

Paul divides his subject into two parts. Verses 15–18 are negative, teaching that the law did not annul the promise of God. Verses 19–22 are positive, teaching that the law illumined God's promise and actually made it indispensable. The first part Paul enforces by an illustration from human affairs, and the second by answering two questions.

1. THE LAW DOES NOT ANNUL THE PROMISE OF GOD (verses 15–18)

The apostle begins the paragraph (verse 15): *To give a human example*. Better, 'let me give you an everyday illustration' (JBP). This illustration is taken from the realm of human promises, not a business contract but a will, what we sometimes call a man's 'last will and testament'. The Greek word in verses 15 and 17 (*diathēkē*) is translated 'covenant' in the Authorized Version because it is used in the Septuagint for the covenants of God. But in classical Greek and the Papyri it was in common use for a will, and is so translated here by the Revised Standard Version. (*Cf.* Heb. 9:15–17, where the two ideas of a covenant and a will are also linked together.)

The point Paul is making is that the wishes and promises which are expressed in a will are unalterable. It is true that in Roman law, as in English law today, a man could change his will, either by making a new one or by adding codicils. For this reason Paul may be referring to ancient Greek law by which a will, once executed and ratified, could not be revoked or even modified. Or he may be saying that it cannot be altered or annulled by somebody else. It certainly cannot be altered by anybody after the testator has died. Whatever the precise legal background may be, it is an *a fortiori* argument, that if a *man's* will cannot be set aside or added to, much more are the promises of *God* immutable.

To what divine promise is he alluding? God promised an inheritance to Abraham and his posterity. Paul knew perfectly well that the immediate, literal reference of this promise was to the land of Canaan, which God was going to give to Abraham's physical descendants. But he also knew that this did not exhaust its meaning; nor was it the ultimate reference in God's mind. Indeed, it could not have been, for God said that in Abraham's seed all the families of the earth would be blessed, and how could the whole world be blessed through Jews living in the land of Canaan? Paul realized that both the 'land' which was promised and the 'seed' to whom it was promised were ultimately spiritual. God's purpose was not just to give the land of Canaan to the Jews, but to give salvation (a spiritual inheritance) to believers who are in Christ. Further, Paul argues, this truth was implicit in the word God used, which was not the plural 'children' or 'descendants', but the singular 'seed' or 'posterity', a collective noun referring to Christ and to all those who are in Christ by faith (verse 16).

Such was God's promise. It was free and unconditional. As we might say, there were 'no strings attached'. There were no works to do, no laws to obey, no merit to establish, no conditions to fulfil. God simply said, 'I will give you a seed. To your seed I will give the land, and in your seed all the nations of the earth will be blessed.' His promise was like a will, freely giving the inheritance to a future generation. And like a human will, this divine promise is unalterable. It is still in force today, for it has never been rescinded. God does not make promises in order to break them. He has never annulled or modified His will.

We are now ready to consider verse 17: *This*, Paul continues, *is what I mean: the law, which came four hundred and thirty years afterward, does not annul a covenant previously ratified by God, so as to make the promise void.* If the Judaizers were right, our Christian inheritance (justification) is given to those who keep the law; and if it is 'by the law, it is no longer by promise', because you cannot have it both ways. *But God gave it to Abraham by a promise* (verse 18). Notice that He 'gave' it. The Greek word *kecharistai* emphasizes both that it is a free gift (a gift of *charis*, 'grace') and that it has been given for good (the perfect tense). God has not gone back on His promise. It is as binding as a man's will; indeed, more so. So every sinner who trusts in Christ crucified for salvation, quite apart from any merit or good works, receives the blessing of eternal life and thus inherits the promise of God made to Abraham.

2. THE LAW ILLUMINES THE PROMISE OF GOD AND MAKES IT INDISPENSABLE (verses 19–22)

Paul now explains the true function of God's law in relation to His promise by asking and answering two questions.

Question 1: 'Why then the law?' (verses 19, 20)

One can almost hear the indignant expostulation of one of the Judaizers, saying something like this: 'Really, Paul, you are the limit! If it is through faith only that a man is in Christ and becomes a beneficiary of God's promise to Abraham, what is the point of the law? Your theology so fuses Abraham and Christ, that you squeeze out Moses and the law altogether. There's no room for the law in your gospel. You wicked, turbulent fellow, your message is akin to blasphemy. You are "teaching men everywhere against . . . the law"' (Acts 21:28).

But Paul had his answer ready. The Judaizers misunderstood and misrepresented his position. He was far from declaring the law unnecessary, for he was quite clear that it had an essential part to play in the purpose of God. The function of the law was not to bestow salvation, however, but to convince men of their need of it. To quote Andrew Jukes, 'Satan would have us to prove ourselves holy by the law, which God gave to prove us sinners.'

The apostle's own statement of the purpose of the law is given in verse 19: *Why then the law? It was added because of transgressions.* He elaborates this in his Epistle to the Romans: 'through the law comes knowledge of sin' (3:20); 'where there is no law there is no transgression' (4:15); and 'if it had not been for the law, I should not have known sin' (7:7). So the law's main work was to expose sin. It is the law which turns 'sin' into 'transgression', showing it up for what it is, a breach of the holy law of God. 'It was added to make wrongdoing a legal offence' (verse 19, NEB). It was intended to make plain the sinfulness of sin as a revolt against the will and authority of God. And it was added *till the offspring should come to whom the promise had been made* (verse 19). Thus, the law looked on to Christ, Abraham's seed, as the Person through whom transgression would be forgiven.

The rest of verse 19 and verse 20 are acknowledged to be difficult. They have been variously interpreted. The apostle is probably emphasizing the inferiority of the law to the gospel. He says that the law 'was promulgated through angels, and there was an intermediary' (verse 19b, NEB). The activity of angels in connection with the giving of the law is mentioned in Deuteronomy 33:2; Psalm 68:17; Acts 7:53 and Hebrews 2:2. The 'intermediary' is doubtless Moses. So when God gave the law He spoke through angels and through Moses. There were two intermediaries—in Lightfoot's expression, 'a double interposition, a twofold mediation, between the giver and the recipient'.[1] But when God spoke the gospel to Abraham He did it direct, and that is probably the meaning of the phrase *God is one* (verse 20). We can sum it up in the words of Bishop Stephen Neill, 'the promise came to Abraham first-hand from God; and the law comes to the people *third-hand*—God—the angels—Moses the mediator—the people'.[2]

Question 2. 'Is the law then against the promises of God?' (verses 21, 22)

This second question is different from the first in that it seems to be addressed not to Paul by the Judaizers, but to the Judaizers by Paul. He is accusing them of doing just this, of making the law

[1] Lightfoot, p. 144. [2] Neill, p. 44.

contradict the gospel, the promises of God. Their teaching was: 'keep the law and you will gain life.' And they thought they were being practical! Paul denies it. Their position was purely hypothetical: *if a law had been given which could make alive, then righteousness would indeed be by the law* (verse 21). But no such law has been given. Turning from hypothesis to reality, the fact is that nobody has ever kept the law of God. Instead, we sinners break it every day. Therefore, the law cannot justify us.

How, then, is it possible to create a harmony between the law and the promise? Only by seeing that men inherit the promise because they cannot keep the law, and that their inability to keep the law makes the promise all the more desirable, indeed indispensable. Verse 22: *The scripture consigned all things to sin*, for the Old Testament plainly declares the universality of human sin, *e.g.* 'there is none that does good, no, not one' (Ps. 14:3). And Scripture holds every sinner in prison for his sins, in order *that what was promised to faith in Jesus Christ might be given to those who believe*. Luther expresses the matter with his usual forcefulness: 'The principal point . . . of the law . . . is to make men not better but worse; that is to say, it sheweth unto them their sin, that by the knowledge thereof they may be humbled, terrified, bruised and broken, and by this means may be driven to seek grace, and so to come to that blessed Seed (*sc.* Christ).'[1]

To summarize, the Judaizers held falsely that the law annuls the promise and supersedes it; Paul teaches the true function of the law, which is to confirm the promise and make it indispensable.

CONCLUSION

The apostle's categories sound foreign to our ears, and his argument is closely knit. Yet he is expounding here some eternal truths.

a. A truth about God

This could be expressed in the words of a well-known hymn: 'God is working His purpose out as year succeeds to year.' Some people seem to think of the Bible as a trackless jungle, full of contradictions, a tangled undergrowth of unrelated ideas. In fact, it is quite

[1] Luther, p. 316.

the opposite, for one of the chief glories of the Bible is its coherence. The whole Bible from Genesis to Revelation tells the story of God's sovereign purpose of grace, His master-plan of salvation through Christ.

Here the apostle Paul, with a breadth of vision which leaves us far behind, brings together Abraham, Moses and Jesus Christ. In eight short verses he spans about 2,000 years. He surveys practically the whole Old Testament landscape. He presents it like a mountain range, whose highest peaks are Abraham and Moses, and whose Everest is Jesus Christ. He shows how God's promise to Abraham was confirmed by Moses and fulfilled in Christ. He teaches the unity of the Bible, especially the Old and New Testaments.

There is a great need in the church today for a biblical, Christian philosophy of history. Most of us are short-sighted and narrow-minded. We are so preoccupied with current affairs in the twentieth century, that neither the past nor the future has any great interest for us. We cannot see the wood for the trees. We need to step back and try to take in the whole counsel of God, His everlasting purpose to redeem a people for Himself through Jesus Christ. Our philosophy of history must make room not only for the centuries after Christ but for the centuries before Him, not only for Abraham and Moses but for Adam, through whom sin and judgment entered the world, and for Christ, through whom salvation has come. If we include the beginning of history, we must include its consummation also, when Christ returns in power and great glory, to take His power and reign. The God revealed in the Bible is working to a plan. He 'accomplishes all things according to the counsel of his will' (Eph. 1:11).

b. A truth about man

After God gave the promise to Abraham, He gave the law to Moses. Why? Simply because He had to make things worse before He could make them better. The law exposed sin, provoked sin, condemned sin. The purpose of the law was, as it were, to lift the lid off man's respectability and disclose what he is really like underneath—sinful, rebellious, guilty, under the judgment of God, and helpless to save himself.

And the law must still be allowed to do its God-given duty today.

One of the great faults of the contemporary church is the tendency to soft-pedal sin and judgment. Like false prophets we 'heal the wound of God's people lightly' (Je. 6:14; 8:11). This is how Dietrich Bonhoeffer put it: 'It is only when one submits to the law that one can speak of grace . . . I don't think it is Christian to want to get to the New Testament too soon and too directly.'[1] We must never bypass the law and come straight to the gospel. To do so is to contradict the plan of God in biblical history.

Is this not why the gospel is unappreciated today? Some ignore it, others ridicule it. So in our modern evangelism we cast our pearls (the costliest pearl being the gospel) before swine. People cannot see the beauty of the pearl, because they have no conception of the filth of the pigsty. No man has ever appreciated the gospel until the law has first revealed him to himself. It is only against the inky blackness of the night sky that the stars begin to appear, and it is only against the dark background of sin and judgment that the gospel shines forth.

Not until the law has bruised and smitten us will we admit our need of the gospel to bind up our wounds. Not until the law has arrested and imprisoned us will we pine for Christ to set us free. Not until the law has condemned and killed us will we call upon Christ for justification and life. Not until the law has driven us to despair of ourselves will we ever believe in Jesus. Not until the law has humbled us even to hell will we turn to the gospel to raise us to heaven.

[1] *Letters and Papers From Prison*, by Dietrich Bonhoeffer (Fontana, 1959), p. 50.

3:23–29

UNDER THE LAW AND IN CHRIST

NOW before faith came, we were confined under the law, kept under restraint until faith should be revealed. [24] *So that the law was our custodian until Christ came, that we might be justified by faith.* [25] *But now that faith has come, we are no longer under a custodian;* [26] *for in Christ Jesus you are all sons of God, through faith.* [27] *For as many of you as were baptized into Christ have put on Christ.* [28] *There is neither Jew nor Greek, there is neither slave nor free, there is neither male nor female; for you are all one in Christ Jesus.* [29] *And if you are Christ's, then you are Abraham's offspring, heirs according to promise.*

IN Galatians 3:15–22 the apostle Paul reviewed 2,000 years of Old Testament history, from Abraham through Moses to Christ. He also showed how these great biblical names are related to one another in the unfolding purpose of God, how God gave to Abraham a promise, and to Moses a law, and how through Christ He fulfilled the promise which the law had revealed as indispensable. For the law condemned the sinner to death, while the promise offered him justification and eternal life.

Now Paul elaborates his theme and shows that this progression from the promise through the law to the fulfilment of the promise is more than the history of the Old Testament and of the Jewish nation. It is the biography of every man, at least of every Christian man. Everybody is either held captive by the law because he is still awaiting the fulfilment of the promise or delivered from the law because he has inherited the promise. More simply, everybody is living either in the Old Testament or in the New, and derives his religion either from Moses or from Jesus. In the language of this paragraph, he is either 'under law' or 'in Christ'.

God's purpose for our spiritual pilgrimage is that we should pass through the law into an experience of the promise. The tragedy is that so many people separate them by wanting one without the other. Some try to go to Jesus without first meeting Moses. They want to skip the Old Testament, to inherit the promise of justification in Christ without the prior pain of condemnation by the law. Others go to Moses and the law to be condemned, but they stay in this unhappy bondage. They are still living in the Old Testament. Their religion is a grievous yoke, hard to be borne. They have never gone to Christ, to be set free.

Both these stages are depicted here. Verses 23 and 24 describe what we were under the law, and verses 25–29 what we are in Christ.

1. WHAT WE WERE UNDER THE LAW (verses 23, 24)

In a word, we were in bondage. The apostle uses two vivid similes in verses 23 and 24, in which the law is likened first to a prison, in which we were held captive, and then to a tutor, whose discipline was harsh and severe.

a. A prison (verse 23)

Now before faith came, we were confined under the law, kept under restraint. . . . Let us examine the two verbs. The Greek word for 'confined' (*phroureō*) means to 'protect by military guards' (Grimm-Thayer). When applied to a city, it was used both of keeping the enemy out and of keeping the inhabitants in, lest they should flee or desert. It is used in the New Testament of the attempt to keep Paul in Damascus: 'The governor under King Aretas *guarded* the city of Damascus (presumably by posting sentries) in order to seize me,' Paul himself wrote (2 Cor. 11:32). And Luke describes how the Jews 'were *watching* the gates day and night, to kill him' (Acts 9:24). Thus confined to the city, his only possible means of escape was the undignified procedure of being smuggled out by night through a window in the wall, and being lowered to the ground in a basket. The same verb is used metaphorically of God's peace and power (Phil. 4:7; 1 Pet. 1:5), and is here applied to the law. It means to 'hold in custody' (Arndt-Gingrich). The verb 'kept under restraint' (*sungkleiō*) is similar. It means to 'hem in' or 'coop up' (Liddell and Scott). Its only literal use in the New Testament comes in Luke's account of the miraculous catch of fish, when 'they *enclosed* a great shoal of fish' (Lk. 5:6).

So both verbs emphasize that God's law and commandments hold us in prison, and keep us confined, so that we cannot escape. The NEB translation is that 'we were close prisoners in the custody of the law'.

b. A tutor (verse 24)

This is Paul's second metaphorical description of the law. The Greek word is *paidagōgos* and means literally a 'tutor, i.e. a guide and guardian of boys' (Grimm-Thayer). He was usually himself a slave, whose duty it was 'to conduct the boy or youth to and from school, and to superintend his conduct generally' (Arndt-Gingrich). The AV translation 'schoolmaster' is unfortunate, for the *paidagōgos* was not the boy's teacher so much as his disciplinarian. He was often harsh to the point of cruelty, and is usually depicted in ancient drawings with a rod or cane in his hand. J. B. Phillips thinks that the modern equivalent is 'a strict governess'. Paul uses the word again in 1 Corinthians 4:15, saying 'You may have ten thousand *tutors* in Christ, but you have only one father' (NEB). In other words, 'there are plenty of people to discipline you, but I am the only one to love you.' Later in the same chapter he asks: 'Am I to come to you with a rod in my hand (*i.e.* like a *paidagōgos*), or in love and a gentle spirit (*i.e.* like a father)?' (1 Cor. 4:21, NEB).

What do these two similes imply? In what sense is the law like a prison gaoler and a child's disciplinarian or tutor? The law expresses the will of God for His people, telling us what to do and what not to do, and warns us of the penalties of disobedience. Since we have all disobeyed, we have fallen under its just condemnation. We are all 'under sin' (verse 22, AV), and therefore we are all 'under the law' (verse 23). By nature and practice we are 'under a curse' (verse 10), that is 'the curse of the law' (verse 13). Nothing we do can deliver us from its cruel tyranny. Like a gaoler it has thrown us into prison; like a *paidagōgos* it rebukes and punishes us for our misdeeds.

But, thank God, He never meant this oppression to be permanent. He gave the law in His grace in order to make the promise more desirable. So to both descriptions of our bondage here Paul adds a time reference: '*Before faith came*, we were confined under the law, kept under restraint *until faith* should be revealed' (verse 23). Again, 'the law was our custodian *until Christ came*, that we might be justified by faith' (verse 24). These are two ways of saying the same thing, because 'faith' and 'Christ' go together. Both verses tell us that the oppressive work of the law was temporary, and that it was ultimately intended not to hurt but to bless. Its purpose was to shut us up in prison until Christ should set us free, or to put us under tutors until Christ should make us sons.

Only Christ can deliver us from the prison to which the curse of the law has brought us, because He was made a curse for us. Only Christ can deliver us from the law's harsh discipline, because He makes us sons who obey from love for their Father and are no longer naughty children needing tutors to punish them.

2. WHAT WE ARE IN CHRIST (verses 25–29)

Verse 25: *But now that faith has come, we are no longer under a custodian.* Paul's adversative phrase 'but now' underlines that what we are is quite different from what we were. We are no longer 'under the law' in the sense that we are condemned and imprisoned by it. Now we are 'in Christ' (verse 26), united to Him by faith, and so have been accepted by God for Christ's sake, in spite of our grievous law-breaking.

The last four verses of Galatians 3 are full of Jesus Christ. Verse 26: '*in Christ Jesus* you are all sons of God, through faith.' Verse 27: 'For as many of you as were baptized *into Christ* have *put on Christ.*' The New English Bible translates 'put on Christ as a garment'. The reference may be to the *toga virilis*, which a boy would put on when he had entered into manhood, a sign that he had grown up. Verse 28b: 'You are all one *in Christ Jesus.*' Verse 29: 'If you are *Christ's* (*i.e.* 'if you belong to Christ', NEB), then you are Abraham's offspring.' This, then, is what a Christian is. He is 'in Christ', he has been 'baptized into Christ', he has 'put on Christ' and he 'belongs to Christ'.

Paul now unfolds three results of being thus united to Christ.

a. In Christ we are sons of God (verses 26, 27)

God is no longer our Judge, who through the law has condemned and imprisoned us. God is no longer our Tutor, who through the law restrains and chastises us. God is now our Father, who in Christ has accepted and forgiven us. We no longer fear Him, dreading the punishment we deserve; we love Him, with deep filial devotion. We are neither prisoners, awaiting the final execution of our sentence, nor children, minors, under the restraint of a tutor, but sons of God and heirs of His glorious kingdom, enjoying the status and privileges of grown-up sons (which is the only sense in which the New Testament would allow the modern fashion that man has 'come of age').

This sonship of God is 'in Christ'; it is not in ourselves. The doctrine of God as a universal Father was not taught by Christ nor by His apostles. God is indeed the universal Creator, having brought all things into existence, and the universal King, ruling and sustaining all that He has made. But He is the Father only of our Lord Jesus Christ and of those whom He adopts into His family through Christ. If we would be the sons of God, then we must be 'in Christ Jesus . . . through faith' (verse 26), which is a better rendering than the familiar 'by faith in Christ Jesus' (AV). It is through faith that we are in Christ, and through being in Christ that we are sons of God.

Our baptism sets forth visibly this union with Christ. Verse 27: *as many of you as were baptized into Christ have put on Christ.* This cannot possibly mean that the act of baptism itself unites a person to Christ, that the mere administration of water makes him a child of God. We must give Paul credit for a consistent theology. This whole Epistle is devoted to the theme that we are justified through faith, not circumcision. It is inconceivable that Paul should now substitute baptism for circumcision and teach that we are in Christ by baptism! The apostle clearly makes *faith* the means of our union with Christ. He mentions faith five times in this paragraph, but baptism only once. Faith secures the union; baptism signifies it outwardly and visibly. Thus in Christ, by faith inwardly (verse 26) and baptism outwardly (verse 27), we are all sons of God.

b. In Christ we are all one (verse 28)

Literally, 'You are all one person in Christ Jesus' (NEB). In Christ we belong not only to God (as His sons) but to each other (as brothers and sisters). And we belong to each other in such a way as to render of no account the things which normally distinguish us, namely race, rank and sex.

First, *there is no distinction of race*. 'There is neither Jew nor Greek' (verse 28). God called Abraham and his descendants (the Jewish race) in order to entrust to them His unique self-revelation. But when Christ came, God's promise was fulfilled that in Abraham's seed all the families of the earth would be blessed. This includes all nations of every race, colour and language. We are equal, equal in our need of salvation, equal in our inability to earn or deserve it, and equal in the fact that God offers it to us freely in Christ. Once we have received it, our equality is transformed into a fellowship, the brotherhood which only Christ can create.

Secondly, *there is no distinction of rank*. 'There is neither slave nor free.' Nearly every society in the history of the world has developed its class or caste system. Circumstances of birth, wealth, privilege and education have divided men and women from one another. But in Christ snobbery is prohibited and class distinctions are rendered void.

Thirdly, *there is no distinction of sex*. 'There is neither male nor female.' This remarkable assertion of the equality of the sexes was made centuries in advance of the times. Women were nearly always despised in the ancient world, even in Judaism, and not infrequently exploited and ill-treated as well. But here the assertion is made that in Christ male and female are one and equal—and made by Paul, who is ignorantly supposed by many to have been an anti-feminist.

A word of caution must be added. This great statement of verse 28 does not mean that racial, social and sexual distinctions are actually obliterated. Christians are not literally 'colour-blind', so that they do not notice whether a person's skin is black, brown, yellow or white. Nor are they unaware of the cultural and educational background from which people come. Nor do they ignore a person's sex, treating a woman as if she were a man or a man as if he were a woman. Of course every person belongs to a certain race and nation, has been nurtured in a particular culture, and is either male or female. When we say that Christ has abolished these distinctions, we mean not that they do not exist, but that they do not matter. They are still there, but they no longer create any barriers to fellowship. We recognize each other as equals, brothers and sisters in Christ. By the grace of God we would resist the temptation to despise one another or patronize one another, for we know ourselves to be 'all one person in Christ Jesus' (NEB).

c. In Christ we are Abraham's seed (verse 29)

And if you are Christ's, then you are Abraham's offspring, heirs according to promise. We have seen that in Christ we belong to God and to each other. In Christ we also belong to Abraham. We take our place in the noble historical succession of faith, whose outstanding representatives are listed in Hebrews 11. No longer do we feel ourselves to be waifs and strays, without any significance in history, or bits of useless flotsam drifting on the tide of time. Instead, we find our place in the unfolding purpose of God. We are the spiritual seed of our father Abraham, who lived and died 4,000 years ago, for in Christ we have become heirs of the promise which God made to him.

These, then, are the results of being 'in Christ', and they speak with powerful relevance to us today. For our generation is busy developing a philosophy of meaninglessness. It is fashionable nowadays to believe (or to say you believe) that life has no meaning, no purpose. There are many who admit that they have nothing to live for. They do not feel that they belong anywhere, or, if they belong, it is to the group known as 'the unattached'. They class themselves as 'outsiders', 'misfits'. They are without anchor, security or home. In biblical language, they are 'lost'.

To such people comes the promise that in Christ we find ourselves. The unattached become attached. They find their place in eternity (related first and foremost to God as His sons and daughters), in society (related to each other as brothers and sisters in the same family) and in history (related also to the succession of God's people down the ages). This is a three-dimensional attachment which we gain when we are in Christ—in height, breadth and length. It is an attachment in 'height' through reconciliation to the God who, although radical theologians repudiate the concept and we must be careful how we interpret it, is a God 'above' us, transcendent over the universe He has made. Next, it is an attachment in 'breadth', since in Christ we are united to all other believers throughout the world. Thirdly, it is an attachment in 'length', as we join the long, long line of believers throughout the whole course of time.

So conversion, although supernatural in its origin, is natural in its effects. It does not disrupt nature, but fulfils it, for it puts me where I belong. It relates me to God, to man and to history. It enables me to answer the most basic of all human questions, 'Who am I?' and to say, 'In Christ I am a son of God. In Christ I am united to all the redeemed people of God, past, present and future. In Christ I discover my identity. In Christ I find my feet. In Christ I come home.'

CONCLUSION

The apostle has painted a vivid contrast between those who are 'under the law' and those who are 'in Christ', and everybody belongs to the one or the other category. If we are 'under the law', our religion is a bondage. Having no knowledge of forgiveness, we are still, as it were, in custody, like prisoners in gaol or children under tutors. It is sad to be in prison and in the nursery when we could be grown up and free. But if we are 'in Christ', we have been set free. Our religion is characterized by 'promise' rather than by 'law'. We know ourselves related to God, and to all God's other children in space, time and eternity.

We cannot come to Christ to be justified until we have first been to Moses to be condemned. But once we have gone to Moses, and acknowledged our sin, guilt and condemnation, we must not stay there. We must let Moses send us to Christ.

4:1–11

ONCE SLAVES, BUT NOW SONS

I MEAN that the heir, as long as he is a child, is no better than a slave, though he is the owner of all the estate; [2] *but he is under guardians and trustees until the date set by the father.* [3] *So with us; when we were children, we were slaves to the elemental spirits of the universe.* [4] *But when the time had fully come, God sent forth his Son, born of woman, born under the law,* [5] *to redeem those who were under the law, so that we might receive adoption as sons.* [6] *And because you are sons, God has sent the Spirit of his Son into our hearts, crying, 'Abba! Father!'* [7] *So through God you are no longer a slave but a son, and if a son then an heir.*

[8] *Formerly, when you did not know God, you were in bondage to beings that by nature are no gods;* [9] *but now that you have come to know God, or rather to be known by God, how can you turn back again to the weak and beggarly elemental spirits, whose slaves you want to be once more?* [10] *You observe days, and months, and seasons, and years!* [11] *I am afraid I have laboured over you in vain.*

WE have seen how in Galatians 3 the apostle Paul surveyed 2,000 years of Old Testament history. In particular, he showed the relation between three of the great figures of biblical history—Abraham, Moses and Jesus Christ. He explained how God gave Abraham a promise to bless all the families of the earth through his posterity; how He then gave Moses a law which, far from annulling the promise, actually made it more necessary and urgent; and how the promise was fulfilled in Christ, so that everyone whom the law drives to Christ inherits the promise which God made to Abraham.

Now in Galatians 4:1–11 Paul rehearses the same history again, contrasting man's condition under the law (verses 1–3) with his condition when he is in Christ (verses 4–7), and basing on this contrast an impassioned appeal about the Christian life (verses 8–11). His sequence of thought might be summarized thus: 'Once we were slaves. Now we are sons. How, then, can we turn back to the old slavery?'

1. MAN'S CONDITION UNDER THE LAW (verses 1–3)

Under the law, Paul says, men were like an heir during his childhood or minority. Let us picture a boy who is the heir to a great estate. One day it will all be his. Indeed, it is already his by promise, but not yet in experience because he is still a child. During his minority, although he is lord of all the estate by title, yet 'he is no better off than a slave' (NEB). He is put 'under guardians and trustees' (RSV, NEB), who act as the 'controllers of his person and property'.[1] They order him about, direct and discipline him. He is under restraint. He has no liberty. Because he is the heir he is, in fact, the lord; but while he is a child, he is no better than a slave. Moreover, he will remain in this bondage 'until the date set by the father' (verse 2).

'So with us,' Paul continues (verse 3). Even in Old Testament days, before Christ came and when we were under the law, we were heirs—heirs of the promise which God made to Abraham. But we had not yet inherited the promise. We were like children during the years of their minority; our childhood was a form of bondage.

What was this bondage? We know, of course, that it was a bondage to the law, for the law was 'our custodian' (3:24) and from it we needed to be 'redeemed' (4:5). But here the law appears to be equated with 'the elemental spirits of the universe' (verse 3). And in verse 9 these 'elemental spirits' are called 'weak and beggarly'—'weak' because the law has no strength to redeem us, and 'beggarly' because it has no wealth with which to bless us.

What are these 'elemental spirits'? The Greek word is *stoicheia*, 'elements'. Broadly speaking, in Greek as in English, the word 'elements' has two meanings. First, it can be used in the sense of 'elementary' things, the letters of the alphabet, the ABC which we learn at school. It occurs in this sense in Hebrews 5:12. If this is Paul's meaning here, then he is likening the Old Testament period to the rudimentary education of the people of God, which was completed by further education when Christ came. The margin of the New English Bible takes it thus as 'elementary ideas belonging to this world' and J. B. Phillips as 'basic moral principles'. Such a

[1] Lightfoot, p. 166.

translation is certainly appropriate to the childhood metaphor which Paul is developing, but on the other hand an elementary stage of education is not exactly a 'bondage'.

The second way in which the word 'elements' can be interpreted is, as in the Revised Standard Version and New English Bible, 'the elemental spirits of the universe'. These were often associated in the ancient world with either the physical elements (earth, fire, air and water) or with the heavenly bodies (the sun, the moon and the stars), which control the seasonal festivals observed on earth. This fits in with verse 8, where we are said to have been 'in bondage to beings that by nature are no gods', namely demons or evil spirits.

But how can a bondage to the law be called a bondage to evil spirits? Is Paul suggesting that the law was an evil design of Satan? Of course not. He has told us that the law was given to Moses by God not Satan, and mediated through angels (3:19), good spirits, not bad. What Paul means is that the devil took this good thing (the law) and twisted it to his own evil purpose, in order to enslave men and women. Just as during a child's minority his guardian may ill-treat and even tyrannize him in ways which his father never intended, so the devil has exploited God's good law, in order to tyrannize men in ways God never intended. God intended the law to reveal sin and to drive men to Christ; Satan uses it to reveal sin and to drive men to despair. God meant the law as an interim step to man's justification; Satan uses it as the final step to his condemnation. God meant the law to be a stepping-stone to liberty; Satan uses it as a cul-de-sac, deceiving his dupes into supposing that from its fearful bondage there is no escape.

2. GOD'S ACTION THROUGH CHRIST (verses 4–7)

Verse 4: *But when the time had fully come....* Man's bondage under the law continued for about 1,300 years. It was a long and arduous minority. But at last the fullness of time arrived (*cf.* Mk. 1:15)—the date set by the Father when the children should attain their majority, be freed from their guardians and inherit the promise.

Why is the period of Christ's coming termed 'the fulness of the time' (AV)? Various factors combined to make it such. For instance, it was the time when Rome had conquered and subdued the known inhabited earth, when Roman roads had been built to facilitate travel and Roman legions had been stationed to guard them. It was also the time when the Greek language and culture had given a certain cohesion to society. At the same time, the old mythological gods of Greece and Rome were losing their hold on the common people, so that the hearts and minds of men everywhere were hungry for a religion that was real and satisfying. Further, it was the time when the law of Moses had done its work of preparing men for Christ, holding them under its tutelage and in its prison, so that they longed ardently for the freedom with which Christ could make them free.

When this fullness of time had come, God did two things.

First, God sent His Son. Verses 4, 5: *When the time had fully come, God sent forth his Son, born of woman, born under the law, to redeem those who were under the law, so that we might receive adoption as sons.* Notice that God's purpose was both to 'redeem' and to 'adopt'; not just to rescue from slavery, but to make slaves into sons.[1] We are not told here how the redemption was achieved, but we know from Galatians 1:4 that it was by the death of Christ and from 3:13 that this death was a 'curse-bearing' death. What is emphasized in these verses is that the one whom God sent to accomplish our redemption was perfectly qualified to do so. He was God's Son. He was also born of a human mother, so that He was human as well as divine, the one and only God-man. And He was born 'under the law', that is, of a Jewish mother, into the Jewish nation, subject to the Jewish law. Throughout His life He submitted to all the requirements of the law. He succeeded where all others before and since have failed: He perfectly fulfilled the righteousness of the law. So the divinity of Christ, the humanity of Christ and the righteousness of Christ uniquely qualified Him to be man's redeemer. If He had not been man, He could not have redeemed men. If He had not been a righteous man, He could not have redeemed unrighteous men. And if He had not been God's Son, He could not have redeemed men for God or made them the sons of God.

Secondly, God sent His Spirit. Verse 6: *And because you are sons, God has sent the Spirit of his Son into our hearts, crying, 'Abba! Father!'* The

[1] 'The metaphor comes from the Graeco-Roman (but not Jewish) legal device whereby a wealthy childless man might take into his family a slave youth who thus, by a great stroke of fortune, ceased to be a slave and became a son and heir' (Hunter, p. 33).

Greek verbs translated 'sent forth' (verse 4) and 'has sent' (verse 6) are the same word and in the same tense (*exapesteilen*). There was, therefore, a double sending forth from God the Father. Observe the Trinitarian reference. First, God sent His Son into the world; secondly, He sent His Spirit into our hearts. And, entering our hearts, the Spirit immediately began to cry 'Abba! Father!', or, as the parallel passage in Romans 8:15, 16 puts it: 'When we cry, "Abba! Father!" it is the Spirit himself bearing witness with our spirit that we are children of God.' 'Abba' is an Aramaic diminutive for 'Father'. It is the word that Jesus Himself used in intimate prayer to God. J. B. Phillips renders it: 'Father, dear Father.' Thus, God's purpose was not only to secure our sonship by His Son, but to assure us of it by His Spirit. He sent His Son that we might have the *status* of sonship, and He sent His Spirit that we might have an *experience* of it. This comes through the affectionate, confidential intimacy of our access to God in prayer, in which we find ourselves assuming the attitude and using the language not of slaves, but of sons.

So the indwelling presence of the Holy Spirit, witnessing to our sonship and prompting our prayers, is the precious privilege of all God's children. It is 'because you are sons' (verse 6) that God has sent the Spirit of His Son into our hearts. No other qualification is needed. There is no need to recite some formula, or strive after some experience, or fulfil some extra condition. Paul says to us clearly that *if* we are God's children, and *because* we are God's children, God has sent His Spirit into our hearts. And the way He assures us of our sonship is not by some spectacular gift or sign, but by the quiet inward witness of the Spirit as we pray.

Verse 7: *So*, Paul concludes this stage of his argument, . . . *you are no longer a slave but a son, and if a son then an heir*. And this changed status is *through God*. What we are as Christians, as sons and heirs of God, is not through our own merit, nor through our own effort, but 'through God', through His initiative of grace, who first sent His Son to die for us and then sent His Spirit to live in us.

3. THE APPEAL OF THE APOSTLE (verses 8-11)

Again Paul contrasts what once we were with what we have become. But this time the contrast is painted in fresh colours, in terms of our knowledge of God. Verse 8: *Formerly, . . . you did not know God.* Verse 9: *but now . . . you have come to know God, or rather* (since the initiative was God's) *to be known by God.* Our bondage was to evil spirits, owing to our ignorance of God; our sonship consists in the knowledge of God, knowing Him and being known by Him, in the intimacy of a personal communion with God which Jesus called 'eternal life' (Jn. 17:3).

Now comes the apostle's appeal. His argument is this: 'If you were a slave and are now a son, if you did not know God but have now come to know Him and to be known by Him, how can you turn back again to the old slavery? How can you allow yourself to be enslaved by the very elemental spirits from whom Jesus Christ has rescued you?' Verse 10: *You observe days, and months, and seasons, and years!* In other words, your religion has degenerated into an external formalism. It is no longer the free and joyful communion of children with their Father; it has become a dreary routine of rules and regulations. And Paul adds sorrowfully: *I am afraid I have laboured over you in vain* (verse 11). He fears that all the time and trouble he has spent over them has been wasted. Instead of growing in the liberty with which Christ had set them free, they have slipped back into the old bondage.

Oh, the folly of these Galatians! We can certainly understand the language of the Prodigal Son, who came to his father and said 'I am no longer worthy to be called your son; treat me as one of your hired servants' or 'slaves'. But how can anyone be so foolish as to say: 'You have made me your son; but I would rather be a slave'? It is one thing to say 'I do not deserve it'; it is quite another to say 'I do not desire it; I prefer slavery to sonship'. Yet that was the folly of the Galatians, under the influence of their false teachers.

CONCLUSION

We may learn from this passage both what the Christian life is and how to live it.

a. What the Christian life is

The Christian life is the life of sons and daughters; it is not the life of slaves. It is freedom, not bondage. Of course, we are slaves of

God, of Christ, and of one another.[1] We belong to God, to Christ, to one another, and we love to serve those to whom we belong. But this kind of service is freedom. What the Christian life is not, is a bondage to the law, as if our salvation hung in the balance and depended on our meticulous and slavish obedience to the letter of the law. As it is, our salvation rests upon the finished work of Christ, on His sin-bearing, curse-bearing death, embraced by faith.

Yet so many religious people are in bondage to their religion! They are like John Wesley in his post-graduate Oxford days in the Holy Club. He was the son of a clergyman and already a clergyman himself. He was orthodox in belief, religious in practice, upright in conduct and full of good works. He and his friends visited the inmates of the prisons and work-houses of Oxford. They took pity on the slum children of the city, providing them with food, clothing and education. They observed Saturday as the Sabbath as well as Sunday. They went to church and to Holy Communion. They gave alms, searched the Scriptures, fasted and prayed. But they were bound in the fetters of their own religion, for they were trusting in themselves that they were righteous, instead of putting their trust in Jesus Christ and Him crucified. A few years later, John Wesley (in his own words) came to 'trust in Christ, in Christ only for salvation' and was given an inward assurance that his sins had been taken away. After this, looking back to his pre-conversion experience, he wrote: 'I had even then the faith of a *servant*, though not that of a son.'[2] Christianity is a religion of sons, not slaves.

b. How to live the Christian life

The way to live the Christian life is to remember who and what we are. The essence of Paul's message here is: 'Once you were slaves. Now you are sons. So how can you revert to the old slavery?' His question is an astonished, indignant expostulation. It is not impossible to turn back to the old life; the Galatians had in fact done it. But it is preposterous to do so. It is a fundamental denial of what we have become, of what God has made us if we are in Christ.

The way for us to avoid the Galatians' folly is to heed Paul's words. Let God's Word keep telling us who and what we are if we

[1] See, *e.g.*, Rom. 6:22; 1 Cor. 7:22, 23; 2 Cor. 4:5.

[2] Footnote added later to the entry for 29 February 1738.

are Christians. We must keep reminding ourselves what we have and are in Christ. One of the great purposes of daily Bible reading, meditation and prayer is just this, to get ourselves correctly orientated, to remember who and what we are. We need to say to ourselves: 'Once I was a slave, but God has made me His son and put the Spirit of His Son into my heart. How can I turn back to the old slavery?' Again: 'Once I did not know God, but now I know Him and have come to be known by Him. How can I turn back to the old ignorance?'

By the grace of God we must determine to remember what once we were and never to return to it; to remember what God has made us and to conform our lives to it.

A good example of this is John Newton. He was an only child and lost his mother when he was seven years old. He went to sea at the tender age of eleven and later became involved, in the words of one of his biographers, 'in the unspeakable atrocities of the African slave trade'. He plumbed the depths of human sin and degradation. When he was twenty-three, on 10 March 1748, when his ship was in imminent peril of foundering in a terrific storm, he cried to God for mercy, and he found it. He was truly converted, and he never forgot how God had had mercy upon him, a former blasphemer. He sought diligently to remember what he had previously been, and what God had done for him. In order to imprint it on his memory, he had written in bold letters and fastened across the wall over the mantelpiece of his study the words of Deuteronomy 15:15: 'Thou shalt remember that thou wast a bondman (a slave) in the land of Egypt, and the Lord thy God redeemed thee.'

If only we remembered these things, what we once were and what we now are, we would have an increasing desire within us to live accordingly, to be what we are, namely sons of God set free by Christ.

4:12–20

THE RELATION BETWEEN PAUL AND THE GALATIANS

BRETHREN, I beseech you, become as I am, for I also have become as you are. You did me no wrong; [13] *you know it was because of a bodily ailment that I preached the gospel to you at first;* [14] *and though my condition was a trial to you, you did not scorn or despise me, but received me as an angel of God, as Christ Jesus.* [15] *What has become of the satisfaction you felt? For I bear you witness that, if possible, you would have plucked out your eyes and given them to me.* [16] *Have I then become your enemy by telling you the truth?* [17] *They* (that is, the false teachers) *make much of you, but for no good purpose; they want to shut you out, that you may make much of them.* [18] *For a good purpose it is always good to be made much of, and not only when I am present with you.* [19] *My little children, with whom I am again in travail until Christ be formed in you!* [20] *I could wish to be present with you now and to change my tone, for I am perplexed about you.*

IF in our study thus far we have thought of Paul merely as a scholar with massive intellectual powers, all head and no heart, this paragraph will correct our first impression. For here Paul appeals to the Galatians with deep feeling and immense tenderness. First, he calls them his 'brethren' in verse 12; then at the end of the paragraph, in verse 19, his 'little children'—a designation of which the apostle John was very fond. He even goes on to liken himself to their mother, who is 'in labour' over them until Christ is formed in them. In Galatians 1–3 we have been listening to Paul the apostle, Paul the theologian, Paul the defender of the faith; but now we are hearing Paul the man, Paul the pastor, Paul the passionate lover of souls.

1. PAUL'S APPEAL (verse 12)

We begin with the simple monosyllables of verse 12 as they are given us in the Authorized Version: 'Be as I am; for I am as ye are.'

Three of the four verbs in this sentence are printed in italics in the Authorized Version, because they are not in the original. In the Greek sentence there is only one verb—the first. We could literally translate, 'Become as I, for I as you.' Or, 'Become like me, for I like you.' What did Paul mean?

a. Become like me

In the context, following his agonized complaint that the Galatians were turning back to the old bondage from which Christ had redeemed them, this appeal can mean only one thing. Paul longed for them to become like him in his Christian faith and life, to be delivered from the evil influence of the false teachers, and to share his convictions about the truth as it is in Jesus, about the liberty with which Christ has made us free. He wanted them to become like himself in his Christian freedom. He expressed a similar sentiment to King Agrippa when the latter said, 'In a short time you think to make me a Christian!' Paul replied, 'Whether short or long, I would to God that not only you but also all who hear me this day might become such as I am—except for these chains' (Acts 26:28, 29). In other words, Paul said to the king: 'I do not want you to become a prisoner like me; but I do want you to become a Christian like me.' All Christians should be able to say something like this, especially to unbelievers, namely that we are so satisfied with Jesus Christ, with His freedom, joy and salvation, that we want other people to become like us.

b. Because I . . . like you

In the light of the verses which follow, it seems that the verb to be supplied must be in the past tense, *i.e.* 'Become as I am, for I also *have become* as you are.' The reference is probably to his visits to them. When Paul came to them in Galatia, he did not keep his distance or stand on his dignity, but became like them. He put himself in their place and identified himself with them. Although he was a Jew, he became like the Gentiles they were. This was in accordance with his principle stated in 1 Corinthians 9:20–22: 'To the Jews I became as a Jew, in order to win Jews. . . . To those outside the law I became as one outside the law . . . that I might win those outside the law. To the weak I became weak, that I might win the weak. I have become all things to all men, that I might by all means save some.'

Embedded here is a principle of far-reaching importance for ministers, missionaries and other Christian workers. It is that, in seeking to win other people for Christ, our end is to make them like us, while the means to that end is to make ourselves like them. If they are to become one with us in Christian conviction and experience, we must first become one with them in Christian compassion. We must be able to say with the apostle Paul: 'I became like you; now you become like me.'

This succinct appeal introduces the rest of the paragraph in which Paul writes both of their attitude to him (verses 13–16) and of his attitude to them (verses 17–20). It is a most enlightening passage, not only because in it we catch a glimpse of Paul the evangelist and pastor, but because we learn the proper relations which should exist today between minister and congregation, between the people and their pastor. In each section Paul draws a contrast. First (verses 13–16), he contrasts their attitude to him in the past, when he visited them, with their attitude to him now, as he is writing to them. Secondly (verses 17–20), he contrasts his attitude to them with the attitude adopted towards them by the false teachers.

2. THE GALATIANS' ATTITUDE TO PAUL (verses 12b–16)

Verse 12b: *You did me no wrong.* Paul has no complaint about their former treatment of him. On the contrary, their behaviour then had been exemplary.

What had happened when he visited Galatia? He reminds them in verse 13 that he had first preached the gospel to them 'through infirmity of the flesh' (AV) or 'because of a bodily ailment' (RSV). We do not know for certain what he meant. Luke says nothing in the Acts about illness being the cause of Paul's visit to the Galatian cities. But presumably, unless he had an attack of some chronic condition, he caught an infection on his way to Galatia, which detained him there. Probably this disease, whatever it was, is the same as the 'thorn' of 2 Corinthians 12:7, which was also 'in the flesh' (that is, in his body) and an *astheneia*, a physical weakness or infirmity. Some people have guessed that Paul caught malaria in the mosquito-infested swamps of coastal Pamphylia, at the time when

John Mark lost his nerve and returned home (Acts 13:13). If so, he would quite naturally have headed north and climbed on to the invigorating mountainous plateau of Galatia. But when he arrived in Galatia, he was in the grip of a great fever. Whatever the disease was, it evidently had unpleasant and unsightly symptoms. It seems to have disfigured him in some way. Further, if we read verse 15 in its context, it appears that his illness affected his eyesight, so that, if it had been possible, the Galatians would have plucked out their own eyes and given them to him. And, indeed, there is other evidence in the New Testament to suggest that Paul may have suffered from some form of ophthalmia.[1]

All this, Paul's physical weakness and disfigurement, was a great trial to the Galatians. Verse 14 should read not '*my* temptation which was in my flesh' (AV), but '*your* temptation . . .'. That is, 'my condition was a trial to you' (RSV). The Galatians had been tempted to despise and reject Paul, to treat him with what Bishop Lightfoot calls 'contemptuous indifference' and even 'active loathing'.[2] But, Paul says, 'you resisted any temptation to show scorn or disgust at the state of my poor body' (NEB). Instead of rejecting him, they 'received' him. Indeed, he continues, *you . . . received me as an angel of God, as Christ Jesus* (verse 14).

This is an extraordinary expression. It is another plain indication of Paul's self-conscious apostolic authority. He sees nothing incongruous about the Galatians receiving him as if he were one of God's angels, or as if he were Christ Jesus, God's Son. He does not rebuke the Galatians for paying an exaggerated deference to him, as he did when the crowd attempted to worship him in Lystra, one of the Galatian cities (Acts 14:8–18). On that occasion, after Paul had healed a congenital cripple, the pagan multitude cried out, 'The gods have come down to us in the likeness of men!' Priest and people tried to sacrifice oxen to Paul and Barnabas, until they rebuked and stopped them. Here, however, Paul does not rebuke them for receiving him as if he were God's angel or God's Christ. Although personally he knew that he was only their fellow-sinner, indeed 'the foremost of sinners' (1 Tim. 1:15), yet officially he was an apostle of Jesus Christ, invested with the authority of Christ and sent on a mission by Christ. So they were quite right to receive him 'as an angel of God', since he was one of God's messengers, and 'as

[1] *E.g.* Acts 23:1–5; Gal. 6:11.

[2] Lightfoot, p. 175.

Christ Jesus', since he came to them on the authority of Christ and with the message of Christ. The apostles of Christ were His personal delegates. Of such it was said in those days that 'the one sent by a person is as this person himself'. Christ Himself had anticipated this. Sending out His apostles, He said: 'He who receives you receives me' (Mt. 10:40). So, in receiving Paul, the Galatians quite rightly received him as Christ, for they recognized him as an apostle or delegate of Christ.

But that was some time ago. Now the situation has changed. Verse 15: *What has become of the satisfaction you felt?* They had been so pleased, so proud, to have Paul among them in those days. Verse 16: *Have I then become your enemy by telling you the truth?* A complete *volte-face* had taken place. The one they had received as God's angel, as God's Son, they now regarded as their enemy! Why? Simply because he had been telling them some painful home truths, rebuking them, scolding them, expostulating with them for deserting the gospel of grace and turning back again to bondage.

There is an important lesson here. When the Galatians recognized Paul's apostolic authority, they treated him as an angel, as Christ Jesus. But when they did not like his message, he became their enemy. How fickle they were, and foolish! An apostle's authority does not cease when he begins to teach unpopular truths. We cannot be selective in our reading of the apostolic doctrine of the New Testament. We cannot, when we like what an apostle teaches, defer to him as an angel, and when we do not like what he teaches, hate him and reject him as an enemy. No, the apostles of Jesus Christ have authority in everything they teach, whether we happen to like it or not.

3. PAUL'S ATTITUDE TO THE GALATIANS (verses 17–20)

Paul now draws a contrast between the attitude of the false teachers to the Galatians and his own attitude to them.

Take the false teachers' attitude first. Verse 17: *They make much of you.* It is not quite certain what Paul means, because this verb is variously translated in the different versions. But he seems to be accusing the false teachers of flattering the Galatians insincerely. In order to win them to their perverted gospel, the false teachers fawned on them and fussed over them. So Paul adds (verse 18): *For a good purpose it is always good to be made much of*. But the false teachers were not sincere in their devotion to the Galatians. Their real motive was that *they want to shut you out* (verse 17), that is, to exclude you from Christ and from the freedom that is in Christ; and they want to do it, in order *that you may make much of them*. When Christianity is seen as freedom in Christ (which it is), Christians are not in subservience to their human teachers, because their ambition is to become mature in Christ. But when Christianity is turned into a bondage to rules and regulations, its victims are inevitably in subjection, tied to the apron-strings of their teachers, as in the Middle Ages.

Paul's attitude to the Galatians was quite different from that of the false teachers. In verse 19 he calls them 'my little children' and likens himself to their mother. But is not this to tie them to his apron-strings? No. The point of the mother-metaphor is not to illustrate their dependence on him, but his travail for them. Verse 19: *My little children, with whom I am again in travail until Christ be formed in you!* He is not satisfied that Christ *dwells* in them; he longs to see Christ *formed* in them, to see them transformed into the image of Christ, 'until you take the shape of Christ' (NEB). Indeed, in ardent desire and prayer he agonizes over them to this end. He likens his pain to the pangs of childbirth. He had been in labour over them previously at the time of their conversion, when they were brought to birth; now their backsliding has caused him another confinement. He is in labour again. The first time there had been a miscarriage; this time he longs that Christ will be truly formed in them. The Arndt-Gingrich *Lexicon* quotes examples of the medical use of this verb for 'the formation of an embryo'. The picture is a bit confused, but, as Dr. Alan Cole rightly says, Paul 'is not giving us a lecture on embryology'.[1] Rather is he expressing his deep and sacrificial love for the Galatians, his longing to see them conformed to the image of Christ. He is 'perplexed' about them (verse 20), at his wits' end (see NEB). He wishes he could visit them now and change his tone, 'from severity to gentleness'.[2]

The difference between Paul and the false teachers should now be clear. The false teachers were seeking *themselves* to dominate the Galatians; Paul longed that *Christ* be formed in them. They had a selfish eye to their own prestige and position; Paul was prepared to

[1] Cole, p. 128. [2] Lightfoot, p. 179.

sacrifice himself for them, to be in travail until Christ was formed in them.

CONCLUSION

'It is one of the high excellences of the Epistles of Paul,' wrote John Brown, 'that they embody a perfect directory for the Christian minister.'[1] In particular, we may learn from this paragraph the reciprocal relationship which should exist between the people and their pastor, between the minister and the congregation. Of course the Christian pastor is not an apostle of Jesus Christ. He has neither the authorization nor the inspiration of an apostle. He may not lay down the law like an apostle. Nor should the congregation defer to him as if he were an apostle. Nevertheless, the Christian minister is called to teach the people the apostolic faith of the New Testament. And if the minister is true to this commission, the people's attitude to him will reflect their attitude to the apostles of Christ, and so to Christ Jesus Himself.

a. The people's attitude to the pastor

How is the congregation's attitude to their minister to be determined? To begin with, it is not to be determined by his personal appearance. He may be ugly, as tradition tells us the apostle Paul was, or good-looking. He may be physically fit, or he may be sickly like Paul when he visited Galatia. He may have a pleasing personality, or be quite unprepossessing. He may have outstanding gifts, or be just a faithful man with no unusual brilliance. But the people should not be swayed in their attitude to him by his outward appearance. They should neither flatter him because they find him attractive, nor despise and reject him because he is not. The Galatians resisted the temptation to let their attitude to Paul be influenced by his personal appearance. So should congregations today.

Next, the people's attitude to the minister should not be determined by their private theological whims. Paul became an 'enemy' to the Galatians simply because they did not like the home truths he was teaching. A congregation should beware of assessing their minister according to their own subjective doctrinal fancies.

[1] Brown, p. 220.

Instead, a congregation's attitude to their minister should be determined by his loyalty to the apostolic message. We have already seen that no minister, however exalted his rank in the visible church, is an apostle of Jesus Christ. Nevertheless, if he is faithful in teaching what the apostles taught, a godly congregation will humbly receive his message and submit to it. They will neither resent nor reject it. Rather, they will welcome it, even with the deference which they would give to an angel of God, to Christ Jesus Himself, because they recognize that the minister's message is not the minister's message, but the message of Jesus Christ.

In the church today there is far too little deference to the apostolic word. Frequently, what interests a contemporary congregation most is the preacher's technique, mannerisms, or voice, how long he preaches for, or whether they can hear him, understand him and agree with him. And often when the sermon is over, they love to criticize it and pull it to pieces.

Certainly, people have cause for criticism if the preacher is unfaithful to his commission, if he makes no attempt to preach biblically, or if he is not himself subject to the apostolic word. But when the minister expounds Scripture, the Word of God, the proper reaction of the congregation should be to receive the message, rather than criticize it—not on the authority of the minister, but on the authority of Christ whose message it is. Most Christian congregations today could be more alert, more humble and more hungry in listening to the exposition of God's Word.

b. The pastor's attitude to the people

Calvin wrote: 'If ministers wish to do any good, let them labour to form Christ, not to form themselves, in their hearers.'[1] The Christian minister should resemble Paul, not the Judaizers. He should be preoccupied with the people's spiritual progress and care nothing for his own prestige. He should not exploit them for his advantage; he should seek to serve them for theirs. He should not use them for his own pleasure, but be willing on their behalf to endure pain. He longs for Christ to be formed in the people; and to this end he is ready to agonize, even to travail in birth. As John Brown comments, 'when such pastors abound, the church must flourish'.[2]

[1] Quoted by Brown, p. 226, note 2. [2] Brown, p. 228.

Notice, finally, the references to Christ in verses 14 and 19. Verse 14: *You . . . received me . . . as Christ Jesus.* Verse 19: *I am again in travail until Christ be formed in you!* What should matter to the people is not the pastor's appearance, but whether *Christ* is speaking through him. And what should matter to the pastor is not the people's favour, but whether *Christ* is formed in them. The church needs people who, in listening to their pastor, listen for the message of Christ, and pastors who, in labouring among the people, look for the image of Christ. Only when pastor and people thus keep their eyes on Christ will their mutual relations keep healthy, profitable and pleasing to almighty God.

4:21–31
ISAAC AND ISHMAEL

TELL *me, you who desire to be under law, do you not hear the law?* [22] *For it is written that Abraham had two sons, one by a slave and one by a free woman.* [23] *But the son of the slave was born according to the flesh, the son of the free woman through promise.* [24] *Now this is an allegory: these women are two covenants. One is from Mount Sinai, bearing children for slavery; she is Hagar.* [25] *Now Hagar is Mount Sinai in Arabia; she corresponds to the present Jerusalem, for she is in slavery with her children.* [26] *But the Jerusalem above is free, and she is our mother.* [27] *For it is written,*

> *'Rejoice, O barren one that dost not bear;*
> *break forth and shout, thou who art not in travail;*
> *for the desolate hath more children*
> *than she who hath a husband.'*

[28] *Now we, brethren, like Isaac, are children of promise.* [29] *But as at that time he who was born according to the flesh persecuted him who was born according to the Spirit, so it is now.* [30] *But what does the scripture say? 'Cast out the slave and her son; for the son of the slave shall not inherit with the son of the free woman.'* [31] *So, brethren, we are not children of the slave but of the free woman.*

MANY people regard this as the most difficult passage in the Epistle to the Galatians. For one thing, it presupposes a knowledge of the Old Testament which few people possess today; there are references in it to Abraham, Sarah, Hagar, Ishmael, Isaac, Mount Sinai and Jerusalem. For another, the argument of Paul is a somewhat technical one; it is the kind which would have been familiar in the Jewish rabbinical schools. It is allegorical, although not arbitrary.

Nevertheless, the message of these verses is right up to date and is specially relevant to religious people. According to verse 21 it is addressed to those *who desire to be under law*. There are many such today. They are not, of course, the Jews or Judaizers to whom Paul was writing, but people whose religion is legalistic, who imagine that the way to God is by the observance of certain rules. There are even professing Christians who turn the gospel into law. They suppose that their relationship to God depends on a strict adherence to regulations, traditions and ceremonies. They are in bondage to them.

To such people Paul says: *You who desire to be under law, do you not hear the law?* (verse 21). With these Judaizers he uses an *argumentum ad hominem*. That is, he meets them and refutes them on their own ground. He exposes the inconsistency, the illogicality of their position. 'You want to be under the law?' he asks. 'Then just listen to the law! For the very law, whose servant you want to be, will be your judge and condemn you.'

There are three stages in the argument of this paragraph. The first is historical, the second allegorical and the third personal. In the historical verses (22, 23) Paul reminds his readers that Abraham had two sons, Ishmael the son of a slave and Isaac the son of a free woman. In the allegorical verses (24–27) he argues that these two sons with their mothers represent two religions, a religion of bondage which is Judaism, and a religion of freedom which is Christianity. In the personal verses (28–31) he applies his allegory to us. If we are Christians, we are not like Ishmael (slaves), but like Isaac (free). Finally, he shows us what to expect if we take after Isaac.

STAGE ONE: THE HISTORICAL BACKGROUND (verses 22, 23)

Verse 22: *it is written that Abraham had two sons.* One of the Jews' loudest and proudest boasts was that they were descended from Abraham, the father and founder of their race. After centuries of confusion following the fall of man, it was to Abraham at last that God plainly revealed Himself. He promised to give to Abraham both the land of Canaan and a posterity as numerous as the stars in the sky and the sand on the seashore. Because of this divine covenant with Abraham and his descendants, the Jews believed themselves to be safe—eternally, inviolably safe.

So John the Baptist needed to say to his Jewish contemporaries: 'do not presume to say to yourselves, "We have Abraham as our father"; for I tell you, God is able from these stones to raise up children to Abraham' (Mt. 3:9). Similarly, when Jesus told the

Jews that if they continued in His word, they would truly be His disciples and would know the truth which would set them free, they replied, '"We are descendants of Abraham, and have never been in bondage to anyone. How is it that you say, 'You will be made free'?" ... Jesus said to them, "If you were Abraham's children" (that is, spiritually as well as physically), "you would do what Abraham did, but now you seek to kill me ...; this is not what Abraham did." ... They said to him, "... we have one Father, even God." Jesus said to them, "If God were your Father, you would love me. ... You are of your father the devil"' (Jn. 8:31–44).

The apostle Paul now elaborates what John the Baptist implied and what Jesus explicitly taught. True descent from Abraham is not physical but spiritual. Abraham's true children are not those with an impeccable Jewish genealogy, but those who believe as Abraham believed and obey as Abraham obeyed. This was the argument of Galatians 3, namely that the blessing promised to Abraham comes not upon Jews as such, the descendants of Abraham according to the flesh, but upon believers, whether Jews or Gentiles (*cf.* Gal. 3:14). Again, 'if you are Christ's, then you are Abraham's offspring, heirs according to promise' (Gal. 3:29; *cf.* Rom. 4:16). We cannot claim to belong to Abraham unless we belong to Christ.

This double descent from Abraham, the false and the true, the false being literal and physical, the true being figurative and spiritual, Paul sees illustrated in Abraham's two sons, Ishmael and Isaac. Both had Abraham as their father, but there were two important differences between them.

The first difference is that they were born of different mothers. Verse 22: *Abraham had two sons, one by a slave and one by a free woman.* Ishmael's mother Hagar was a slave woman, Abraham's servant. Isaac's mother Sarah was a free woman, Abraham's wife. And each boy took after his mother. So Ishmael was born into slavery, but Isaac into freedom.

The second difference is that they were born in different ways. Not, of course, that the biological processes of conception and birth were different, but that different circumstances gave rise to their birth. Verse 23: *the son of the slave was born according to the flesh* (or 'in the course of nature', NEB), *the son of the free woman through promise.* Isaac was not born according to nature, but rather against nature.

His father was a hundred years old and his mother, who had been barren, was over ninety. This is how it is put in Hebrews 11:11: 'By faith Sarah herself received power to conceive, even when she was past the age, since she considered him faithful who had promised.' Notice the word 'promised'. Ishmael was born according to nature, but Isaac against nature, supernaturally, through an exceptional promise of God.

These two differences between Abraham's sons, that Ishmael was born a slave according to nature, while Isaac was born free according to promise, Paul recognizes as 'an allegory'. Everyone is a slave by nature, until in the fulfilment of God's promise he is set free. So everyone is either an Ishmael or an Isaac, either still what he is by nature, a slave, or by the grace of God set free.

STAGE TWO: THE ALLEGORICAL ARGUMENT (verses 24–27)

Although they are historical events, the circumstances of the births of Ishmael and Isaac also stand for a deeply spiritual truth. Verse 24 (NEB): 'the two women stand for two covenants.'

An understanding of the Bible is impossible without an understanding of the two covenants. After all, our Bibles are divided in half, into the Old and New Testaments, meaning the Old and New 'Covenants'. A covenant is a solemn agreement between God and men, by which He makes them His people and promises to be their God. God established the old covenant through Moses and the new covenant through Christ, whose blood ratified it. The old (Mosaic) covenant was based on law; but the new (Christian) covenant, foreshadowed through Abraham and foretold through Jeremiah, is based on promises. In the law God laid the responsibility on men and said 'thou shalt . . ., thou shalt not . . .'; but in the promise God keeps the responsibility Himself and says 'I will . . ., I will . . .'.

In this passage there are not only two covenants mentioned, but two Jerusalems also. Jerusalem, of course, was the capital city which God chose for the land that He gave to His people. It was natural, therefore, that the word 'Jerusalem' should stand for God's people, just as 'Moscow' stands for the Russian people, 'Tokyo' for the Japanese, 'Washington' for the Americans and 'London' for the English.

But who are the people of God? God's people under the old

covenant were the Jews, but His people under the new covenant are Christians, believers. Both are 'Jerusalem', but the old covenant people of God, the Jews, are 'the present Jerusalem', the earthly city, whereas the new covenant people of God, the Christian church, are 'the Jerusalem above', the heavenly. Thus, the two women, Hagar and Sarah, the mothers of Abraham's two sons, stand for the two covenants, the old and the new, and the two Jerusalems, the earthly and the heavenly.

Before considering in greater detail what the apostle writes about these two women, it may be helpful to read the New English Bible version of verses 24 to 27: 'This is an allegory. The two women stand for two covenants. The one bearing children into slavery is the covenant that comes from Mount Sinai: that is Hagar. Sinai is a mountain in Arabia and it represents the Jerusalem of today, for she and her children are in slavery. But the heavenly Jerusalem is the free woman; she is our mother. For Scripture says, "Rejoice, O barren woman who never bore child; break into a shout of joy, you who never knew a mother's pangs; for the deserted wife shall have more children than she who lives with the husband." '

Take Hagar first. As the mother who bore children into slavery, she stands for the covenant from Mount Sinai, the Mosaic law. This is clear, Paul adds in a parenthesis, because 'Sinai is a mountain in Arabia', and the Arabians were known as 'the sons of Hagar'. It is even more clear from the fact that the children of the law, just like Hagar's children, are slaves. So Hagar stands for the covenant of law. She also 'corresponds to the present Jerusalem, for she is in slavery with her children' (verse 25).

But Sarah was different. Verse 26 (NEB): 'But the heavenly Jerusalem is the free woman; she is our mother.' That is, if Hagar, Ishmael's mother the slave woman, stands for the earthly Jerusalem or Judaism, then Sarah, Isaac's mother, being a free woman, stands for the heavenly Jerusalem or the Christian church. And, Paul adds, 'she is our mother'. As Christians we are citizens of 'the Jerusalem above'. We are bound to the living God by a new covenant, and this citizenship is not bondage, but freedom.

Paul goes on (in verse 27) to quote Isaiah 54:1. Its reference to two women, one barren and the other with children, is not to Hagar and Sarah, but to the Jews. The prophet is addressing the exiles in Babylonian captivity. He likens their state in exile, under divine judgment, to that of a barren woman finally deserted by her husband, and their future state after the restoration to that of a fruitful mother with more children than ever. In other words, God promises that His people will be more numerous after their return than they were before. This promise received a literal but partial fulfilment in the restoration of the Jews to the promised land. But its true, spiritual fulfilment, Paul says, is in the growth of the Christian church, since Christian people are the seed of Abraham.

This, then, is the allegory. Abraham had two sons, Ishmael and Isaac, born of two mothers, Hagar and Sarah, who represent two covenants and two Jerusalems. Hagar the slave stands for the old covenant, and her son Ishmael symbolizes the church of the earthly Jerusalem. Sarah the free woman stands for the new covenant, and her son Isaac symbolizes the church of the heavenly Jerusalem. Although superficially similar, because both were sons of Abraham, the two boys were fundamentally different. In the same way, Paul is arguing, it is not enough to claim Abraham as our father. The crucial question concerns who our mother is. If it is Hagar, we are like Ishmael, but if it is Sarah, we are like Isaac.

STAGE THREE: THE PERSONAL APPLICATION (verses 28–31)

Verse 28: *Now we, brethren, like Isaac, are children of promise.* If we are Christians, we are like Isaac, not Ishmael. Our descent from Abraham is spiritual not physical. We are not his sons by nature, but by supernature.

What follows is this: if we are like Isaac, we must expect to be treated as Isaac was treated. The treatment Isaac got from his half-brother Ishmael is the treatment that Isaac's descendants will get from Ishmael's descendants. And the treatment that Isaac got from his father Abraham is the treatment that we must expect from God.

a. We must expect persecution

Verse 29: *But as at that time he who was born according to the flesh persecuted him who was born according to the Spirit, so it is now.* At the ceremony at which Isaac was weaned, when he was probably a boy of three and Ishmael a youth of seventeen, Ishmael ridiculed his little half-brother Isaac. We do not know the details of what happened, because

Ishmael's attitude is described by only one Hebrew verb, probably meaning that he 'laughed' or 'mocked' (Gn. 21:9). Nevertheless, it is clear that Isaac was the object of Ishmael's scorn and derision.

We must expect the same. The persecution of the true church, of Christian believers who trace their spiritual descent from Abraham, is not always by the world, who are strangers unrelated to us, but by our half-brothers, religious people, the nominal church. It has always been so. The Lord Jesus was bitterly opposed, rejected, mocked and condemned by His own nation. The fiercest opponents of the apostle Paul, who dogged his footsteps and stirred up strife against him, were the official church, the Jews. The monolithic structure of the medieval papacy persecuted all Protestant minorities with ruthless, unremitting ferocity. And the greatest enemies of the evangelical faith today are not unbelievers, who when they hear the gospel often embrace it, but the church, the establishment, the hierarchy. Isaac is always mocked and persecuted by Ishmael.

b. We shall receive the inheritance

Verse 30: *But what does the scripture say? 'Cast out the slave and her son; for the son of the slave shall not inherit with the son of the free woman.'* Although Isaac had to endure the scorn of his half-brother Ishmael, it was Isaac who became heir of his father Abraham and received the inheritance. At one stage Abraham wanted Ishmael to be the heir: 'Oh that Ishmael might live in thy sight!' he cried to God. And God replied, 'No, . . . But I will establish my covenant with Isaac' (Gn. 17:18–21). So Sarah asked Abraham to cast out the slave and her son, and God told Abraham to do what Sarah said. For, although He was going to make a nation of the slave woman's son too (that is, Ishmael the father of the Arabians), yet He added 'through Isaac shall your descendants be named' (Gn. 21:10–13).

So it is that the true heirs of God's promise to Abraham are not his children by physical descent, the Jews, but his children by spiritual descent, Christian believers whether Jews or Gentiles. And since it is 'the Scripture' which said 'Cast out the slave and her son', we find the law itself rejecting the law. This verse of Scripture, which the Jews interpreted as God's rejection of the Gentiles, Paul boldly reverses and applies to the exclusion of unbelieving Jews from the inheritance. As J. B. Lightfoot comments, 'the Apostle thus confidently sounds the death-knell of Judaism.'[1]

Such, then, is the double lot of 'Isaacs'—the pain of persecution on the one hand and the privilege of inheritance on the other. We are despised and rejected by men; yet we are the children of God, 'and if children, then heirs, heirs of God and fellow heirs with Christ' (Rom. 8:17). This is the paradox of a Christian's experience. As Paul puts it in 2 Corinthians 6:8–10, we are 'in honour and dishonour, in ill repute and good repute, . . . as sorrowful, yet always rejoicing; as poor, yet making many rich; as having nothing, and yet possessing everything.'

CONCLUSION

This passage teaches us the scintillating glory of being a Christian believer. It involves, among others, two great privileges.

First, *we inherit the promises of the Old Testament.* The true fulfilment of the Old Testament promises is not literal but spiritual. They are fulfilled today not in the Jewish nation, as some dispensationalists hold, nor in the British or Anglo-Saxon people, as the British Israelites teach, but in Christ and in the people of Christ who believe. We Christians are Abraham's seed, who inherit the blessing promised to his descendants (3:29). Like Isaac we are 'children of promise' (verse 28) and 'children . . . of the free woman' (verse 31). We are citizens of the true Jerusalem, 'the Jerusalem above' (verse 26; *cf.* Heb. 12:22; Rev. 3:12; 21:2). We are 'the Israel of God' (Gal. 6:16) and 'the true circumcision' (Phil. 3:3). No doubt we shall be persecuted, but all the promises of God to His people in the Old Testament become ours if we are Christ's.

Secondly, *we experience the grace of God,* His gracious initiative to save us. We have seen that Abraham's two sons and their two mothers stand for the two covenants, the old and the new, and for the two Jerusalems, the earthly and the heavenly. We have also seen that whereas the categories of the old covenant are nature, law and bondage, the categories of the new are promise, the Spirit and freedom. What is the fundamental difference between them? It is this. The religion of Ishmael is a religion of *nature,* of what *man* can do by himself without any special intervention of God. But the religion

[1] Lightfoot, p. 184.

of Isaac is a religion of *grace*, of what *God* has done and does, a religion of divine initiative and divine intervention, for Isaac was born supernaturally through a divine promise. And this is what Christianity is, not 'natural' religion but 'supernatural'. The Ishmaels of this world trust in themselves that they are righteous, the Isaacs trust only in God through Jesus Christ. The Ishmaels are in bondage, because this is what self-reliance always leads to; the Isaacs enjoy freedom, because it is through faith in Christ that men are set free.

So we must seek to be like Isaac, not like Ishmael. We must put our trust in God through Jesus Christ. For only in Christ can we inherit the promises, receive the grace and enjoy the freedom of God.

5:1–12

FALSE AND TRUE RELIGION

FOR *freedom Christ has set us free; stand fast therefore, and do not submit again to a yoke of slavery.*

[2] *Now I, Paul, say to you that if you receive circumcision, Christ will be of no advantage to you.* [3] *I testify again to every man who receives circumcision that he is bound to keep the whole law.* [4] *You are severed from Christ, you who would be justified by the law; you have fallen away from grace.* [5] *For through the Spirit, by faith, we wait for the hope of righteousness.* [6] *For in Christ Jesus neither circumcision nor uncircumcision is of any avail, but faith working through love.* [7] *You were running well; who hindered you from obeying the truth?* [8] *This persuasion is not from him who called you.* [9] *A little yeast leavens the whole lump.* [10] *I have confidence in the Lord that you will take no other view than mine; and he who is troubling you will bear his judgment, whoever he is.* [11] *But if I, brethren, still preach circumcision, why am I still persecuted? In that case the stumbling-block of the cross has been removed.* [12] *I wish those who unsettle you would mutilate themselves!*

THE Epistle to the Galatians is essentially a polemical Epistle, an Epistle in which Paul plunges headlong into controversy because of the introduction into the Galatian churches of erroneous teaching.

And these verses at the beginning of Galatians 5 are in keeping with the tenor of the whole Epistle. It is a paragraph of contrasts in which the apostle sets over against each other two opinions or outlooks, indeed virtually two religions, one false and the other true. He draws the contrast twice, first (verses 1–6) from the standpoint of those who practise these two religions, and secondly (verses 7–12) from the standpoint of those who preach them.

1. BELIEVERS FALSE AND TRUE (verses 1–6)

The best manuscripts divide verse 1 into two separate sentences, so that they are not a single command (as in AV) to 'stand fast . . . in the liberty wherewith Christ hath made us free', but first an assertion (*for freedom Christ has set us free*), followed by a command based upon it (*stand fast therefore, and do not submit again to a yoke of slavery*).

a. The assertion

As the New English Bible puts it, 'Christ set us free, to be free men'. Our former state is portrayed as a slavery, Jesus Christ as a liberator, conversion as an act of emancipation and the Christian life as a life of freedom. This freedom, as the whole Epistle and this context make plain, is not primarily a freedom from sin, but rather from the law. What Christ has done in liberating us, according to Paul's emphasis here, is not so much to set our *will* free from the bondage of sin as to set our *conscience* free from the guilt of sin. The Christian freedom he describes is freedom of conscience, freedom from the tyranny of the law, the dreadful struggle to keep the law, with a view to winning the favour of God. It is the freedom of acceptance with God and of access to God through Christ.

b. The command

Since 'Christ has set us free' and that 'for freedom', we must 'stand fast' in it and not 'submit again to a yoke of slavery'. In other words, we are to enjoy the glorious freedom of conscience which Christ has brought us by His forgiveness. We must not lapse into the idea that we have to win our acceptance with God by our own obedience. The picture seems to be of an ox bowed down by a heavy yoke.[1] Once it has been freed from this crushing yoke, it is able to stand erect again (*cf.* Lv. 26:13).

It is just so in the Christian life. At one time we were under the yoke of the law, burdened by its demands which we could not meet and by its fearful condemnation because of our disobedience. But Christ met the demands of the law for us. He died for our disobedience and thus bore our condemnation in our place. He has 'redeemed us from the curse of the law, having become a curse for us' (3:13). And now He has struck the yoke from our shoulder and

[1] According to Arndt-Gingrich the verb 'do not submit' is passive and means 'to be loaded down with'.

set us free to stand upright. How then can we dream of putting ourselves under the law again and submitting to its cruel yoke?

This, then, is the theme of these verses. Christianity is freedom not bondage. Christ has set us free; so we must stand firm in our freedom.

From the general theme we come to the precise issue in verses 2–4, which is that of circumcision. The false teachers in the Galatian churches, as we have already seen, were saying that Christian converts had to be circumcised. You might think this a very trivial matter. After all, circumcision is only a very minor surgical operation on the body. Why did Paul make so much fuss and bother about it? Because of its doctrinal implications. As the false teachers were pressing it, circumcision was neither a physical operation, nor a ceremonial rite, but a theological symbol. It stood for a particular type of religion, namely salvation by good works in obedience to the law. The slogan of the false teachers was: 'Unless you are circumcised and keep the law, you cannot be saved' (*cf.* Acts 15:1, 5). They were thus declaring that faith in Christ was insufficient for salvation. Circumcision and law-obedience must be added to it. This was tantamount to saying that Moses must be allowed to finish what Christ had begun.

See how Paul describes their position in these verses. They are those who 'receive circumcision' (verses 2, 3), who are therefore 'bound to keep the whole law' (verse 3), since this is what their circumcision commits them to, and who are seeking to 'be justified by the law' (verse 4).

What does Paul say to them? He does not mince his words. On the contrary, he makes a most solemn assertion, beginning *Now I, Paul, say to you* (verse 2). He warns them in three sentences of the serious results of their receiving circumcision: *Christ will be of no advantage to you* (verse 2), *you are severed from Christ* and *you have fallen away from grace* (verse 4). More simply, to add circumcision is to lose Christ, to seek to be justified by the law is to fall from grace. You cannot have it both ways. It is impossible to receive Christ, thereby acknowledging that you cannot save yourself, and then receive circumcision, thereby claiming that you can. You have got to choose between a religion of law and a religion of grace, between Christ and circumcision. You cannot add circumcision (or anything else, for that matter) to Christ as necessary to salvation, because

Christ is sufficient for salvation in Himself. If you add anything to Christ, you lose Christ. Salvation is in Christ alone by grace alone through faith alone.

In verses 5 and 6 the pronoun changes from 'you' to 'we'. Paul has been addressing his readers and warning them of the danger of falling from grace. But now he includes himself and describes true believers, evangelical believers, who stand in the gospel of grace: *For through the Spirit, by faith, we wait for the hope of righteousness. For in Christ Jesus neither circumcision nor uncircumcision is of any avail, but faith working through love* (verses 5, 6). The emphasis in these verses is on faith. Two statements are made about it.

First, 'by faith we wait' (verse 5). What we are waiting for is termed 'the hope of righteousness', the expectation for the future which our justification brings, namely spending eternity with Christ in heaven. For this future salvation we wait. We do not *work* for it; we *wait* for it by faith. We do not strive anxiously to secure it, or imagine that we have to earn it by good works. Final glorification in heaven is as free a gift as our initial justification. So by faith, trusting only in Christ crucified, we wait for it.

Secondly, 'in Christ what matters is faith' (verse 6). Again Paul denies the false teaching. When a person is in Christ, nothing more is necessary. Neither circumcision nor uncircumcision can improve our standing before God. All that is necessary in order to be accepted with God is to be in Christ, and we are in Christ by faith.

A word of caution is needed here. Does this emphasis on faith in Christ mean that we can live and act as we please? Is the Christian life so completely a life of faith that good works and obedience to the law simply do not matter? No. Paul is very careful to avoid giving any such impression. Notice the phrases which I have so far omitted. Verse 5: 'For *through the Spirit*, by faith, we wait for the hope of righteousness.' That is to say, the Christian life is not only a life of faith; it is a life in the Spirit, and the Holy Spirit who indwells us produces good works of love, as the apostle goes on later to explain (verses 22, 23). Verse 6: 'faith *working through love*.' It is not that works of love are added to faith as a second and subsidiary ground of our acceptance with God, but that the faith which saves is a faith which works, a faith which issues in love.

2. TEACHERS FALSE AND TRUE (verses 7–12)

In verses 1–6 the contrast has been between the pronouns 'you' and 'we'—you the false believers who want to add circumcision to faith, and we the true believers who are content with Christ alone and with faith alone. Now the contrast is between 'he', the false teacher 'who is troubling you' (verse 10b), and 'I', the apostle Paul who am teaching you the truth of God.

Verse 7: *You were running well; who hindered you from obeying the truth?* Paul loved to liken the Christian life to a race in the arena. Notice that to 'run well' in the Christian race is not just to believe the truth (as if Christianity were nothing but orthodoxy), nor just to behave well (as if it were just moral uprightness), but to 'obey the truth', applying belief to behaviour. Only he who obeys the truth is an integrated Christian. What he believes and how he behaves are all of a piece. His creed is expressed in his conduct; his conduct is derived from his creed.

Now the Galatians had begun the Christian race, and at first they ran well. They believed the truth that Christ had set them free, and they obeyed it, enjoying the liberty which Christ had given them. But someone had hindered them; an obstacle had been thrown on the track to deviate them from the path. False teachers had contradicted the truth they had first believed. As a result they had forsaken Christ and fallen from grace.

Paul traces the full course of the false teaching, its origin, its effect and its end.

a. Its origin

Verse 8: *This persuasion is not from him who called you.* The false teachers had persuaded the Galatians to abandon the truth of the gospel, but this work of persuasion was not from the God who had called them. For God had called them in grace (Gal. 1:6), whereas the false teachers were propagating a doctrine of merit. This is Paul's first argument: the false teachers' message was inconsistent with the Galatians' call.

b. Its effect

We have already seen that the heresy 'hindered' the Galatians (verse 7), as later Paul is to say that it 'troubled' (verse 10) and 'unsettled' them (verse 12). But now (verse 9) he uses the common proverb, *A little yeast leavens the whole lump*. That is, the error of the false teachers was spreading in the Christian community until the whole church was becoming contaminated. Paul uses the same proverb in 1 Corinthians 5:6. There he applies it to sin in the Christian community, here to false teaching. One of the most serious things about evil and error is that they both spread.

So because of the cause and effect of the false teaching, because it was not from God and because its influence was spreading, Paul was determined to resist it.

c. Its end

Verse 10: *I have confidence in the Lord that you will take no other view than mine; and he who is troubling you will bear his judgment, whoever he is.* Paul is quite sure that error is not going to triumph, but that the Galatians will come to a better mind and that the false teacher, however exalted his rank, will fall under the judgment of God. Indeed, so concerned is Paul about the damage which the false teachers are doing, that he even expresses the wish that they 'would mutilate themselves' (verse 12) or 'make eunuchs of themselves' (NEB) like the priests of the heathen goddess Cybele in Asia Minor. His sentiment sounds to our ears both coarse and malicious. We may be quite sure, however, that it was due neither to an intemperate spirit, nor to a thirst for revenge, but to his deep love for the people of God and the gospel of God. I venture to say that if we were as concerned for God's church and God's Word as Paul was, we too would wish that false teachers might cease from the land.

With verse 11 (*But if I . . .*) Paul turns from them (the false teachers hindering the Galatians) to himself (their true teacher sent from God). It seems that these teachers had dared even to claim Paul as a champion of their views. They were spreading the rumour that Paul also preached and advocated circumcision. The apostle flatly denies it, and goes on to give evidence of the falsity of their claim. Verse 11: *If I, brethren, still preach circumcision, why am I still persecuted? In that case* (*i.e.* if I were still preaching circumcision) *the stumbling-block of the cross has been removed.*

Thus Paul sets himself and the false teachers in stark contrast. They were preaching circumcision; he was preaching Christ and the cross. To preach circumcision is to tell sinners that they can save themselves by their own good works; to preach Christ crucified is to tell them that they cannot and that only Christ can save them through the cross. The message of circumcision is quite inoffensive, popular because flattering; the message of Christ crucified is, however, offensive to human pride, unpopular because unflattering. So to preach circumcision is to avoid persecution; to preach Christ crucified is to invite it. People hate to be told that they can be saved only at the foot of the cross, and they oppose the preacher who tells them so.

Now since he was being persecuted, Paul argues that he was not preaching circumcision. On the contrary, he was preaching Christ crucified, and the stumbling-block of the cross had not been removed. It was the false teachers who were pressing the Galatians to be circumcised, in order to avoid persecution for the cross of Christ (see Gal. 6:12).

Persecution or opposition is a mark of every true Christian preacher. As we saw in Galatians 4:29, the Isaacs of this world are always persecuted by the Ishmaels. The Old Testament prophets found it so, men like Amos, Jeremiah, Ezekiel and Daniel. So did the New Testament apostles. And down the centuries of the Christian church, until and including today, Christian preachers who refuse to distort or dilute the gospel of grace have had to suffer for their faithfulness. The good news of Christ crucified is still a 'scandal' (Greek, *skandalon*, stumbling-block), grievously offensive to the pride of men. It tells them that they are sinners, rebels, under the wrath and condemnation of God, that they can do nothing to save themselves or secure their salvation, and that only through Christ crucified can they be saved. If we preach this gospel, we shall arouse ridicule and opposition. Only if we 'preach circumcision', the merits and the sufficiency of man, shall we escape persecution and become popular.

CONCLUSION

Ours is an age of tolerance. Men love to have the best of both worlds and hate to be forced to choose. It is commonly said that it does not matter what people believe so long as they are sincere, and that it is unwise to clarify issues too plainly or to focus them too sharply.

But the religion of the New Testament is vastly different from this mental outlook. Christianity will not allow us to sit on the fence or live in a haze; it urges us to be definite and decisive, and in particular to choose between Christ and circumcision. 'Circumcision' stands for a religion of *human* achievement, of what man can do by his own good works; 'Christ' stands for a religion of *divine* achievement, of what God has done through the finished work of Christ. 'Circumcision' means law, works and bondage; 'Christ' means grace, faith and freedom. Every man must choose. The one impossibility is what the Galatians were attempting, namely to add circumcision to Christ and have both. No. 'Circumcision' and 'Christ' are mutually exclusive.

Further, this choice has to be made by both the people and the ministers of the church, by those who practise and those who propagate religion. It is either Christ or circumcision that the people 'receive' (verse 2), and either Christ or circumcision that ministers 'preach' (verse 11). In principle, there is no third alternative.

And behind our choice lurks our motive. It is when we are bent on flattering ourselves and others that we choose circumcision. Before the cross we have to humble ourselves.

5:13–15

THE NATURE OF CHRISTIAN FREEDOM

FOR you were called to freedom, brethren; only do not use your freedom as an opportunity for the flesh, but through love be servants of one another. [14] *For the whole law is fulfilled in one word, 'You shall love your neighbour as yourself.'* [15] *But if you bite and devour one another take heed that you are not consumed by one another.*

'FREEDOM' is a word on everybody's lips today. There are many different forms of it, and many different people advocating it and canvassing it. There is the African nationalist who has gained 'Uhuru' for his country—freedom from colonial rule. There is the economist who believes in free trade, the lifting of tariffs. There is the capitalist who dislikes central controls because they hinder free enterprise and the communist who claims to set the proletariat free from capitalist exploitation. There are the famous four freedoms first enunciated by President Roosevelt in 1941, when he spoke of 'freedom of speech everywhere, freedom of worship everywhere, freedom from want everywhere and freedom from fear everywhere'.

What sort of freedom is Christian freedom? Primarily, as we saw in the previous chapter, it is a freedom of conscience. According to the Christian gospel no man is truly free until Jesus Christ has rid him of the burden of his guilt. And Paul tells the Galatians that they had been 'called' to this freedom. It is equally true of us. Our Christian life began not with our decision to follow Christ but with God's call to us to do so. He took the initiative in His grace while we were still in rebellion and sin. In that state we neither wanted to turn from sin to Christ, nor were we able to. But He came to us and called us to freedom.

Paul knew this from his own experience, for God had 'called' him 'through his grace' (1: 15). The Galatians knew it from their experience too, for Paul complained that they were so quickly deserting Him who had 'called' them 'in the grace of Christ' (1:6). Every

Christian knows it also today. If we are Christians, it is not through any merit of our own, but through the gracious calling of God.

'Called to freedom'! This is what it means to be a Christian, and it is tragic that the average man does not know it. The popular image of Christianity today is not freedom at all, but a cruel and cramping bondage. But Christianity is not a bondage; it is a call of grace to freedom. Nor is this the exceptional privilege of a few believers, but rather the common inheritance of all Christians without distinction. That is why Paul adds 'brethren'. Every single Christian brother and sister has been called by God and called to freedom.

What are the implications of Christian freedom? Does it include freedom from every kind of restraint and restriction? Is Christian liberty another word for anarchy? Paul himself was being criticized for teaching this, and it was an easy jibe for his detractors to make. So, having asserted that we have been called to liberty, he immediately sets himself to define the freedom to which we have been called, to clear it of misconceptions and to protect it from irresponsible abuse. In brief, it is freedom from the awful bondage of having to merit the favour of God; it is not freedom from all controls.

1. CHRISTIAN FREEDOM IS NOT FREEDOM TO INDULGE THE FLESH (verse 13)

You were called to freedom, brethren; only do not use your freedom as an opportunity for the flesh. 'The flesh' in the language of the apostle Paul is not what clothes our bony skeleton, but our fallen human nature, which we inherited from our parents and they inherited from theirs, and which is twisted with self-centredness and therefore prone to sin. We are not to use our Christian freedom to indulge this 'flesh', 'as an opportunity for the flesh'. The Greek word here translated 'opportunity' (*aphormē*) is used in military contexts for a place from which an offensive is launched, a base of operations. It therefore means a vantage-ground, and so an opportunity or pretext. Thus our freedom in Christ is not to be used as a pretext for self-indulgence.

Christian freedom is freedom *from* sin, not freedom *to* sin. It is an unrestricted liberty of approach to God as His children, not an unrestricted liberty to wallow in our own selfishness. The New English Bible puts it well: 'You . . . were called to be free men; only do not turn your freedom into licence for your lower nature.' Indeed, such 'liberty', an unbridled licence, is not true liberty at all; it is another and more dreadful form of bondage, a slavery to the desires of our fallen nature. So Jesus said to the Jews: 'every one who commits sin is a slave to sin' (Jn. 8:34), and Paul described us in our pre-conversion state as 'slaves to various passions and pleasures' (Tit. 3:3).

There are many such slaves in our society today. They proclaim their freedom with a loud voice. They speak of free love and a free life; but in reality they are slaves to their own appetites to which they give free rein, simply because they cannot control them.

Christian freedom is very different. Far from having liberty to indulge the flesh, Christians are said to 'have crucified the flesh with its passions and desires' (verse 24). That is to say, we have totally repudiated the claim of our lower nature to rule over us. In vivid imagery which Paul borrows from Jesus, he says that we have 'crucified' it, nailed it to the cross. Now we seek to walk in the Spirit and are promised, if we do, that we shall 'not gratify the desires of the flesh' (verse 16). Instead the Holy Spirit will cause His fruit to ripen in our lives, culminating in self-control (verse 23). We shall consider these verses in greater detail in the next chapter.

2. CHRISTIAN FREEDOM IS NOT FREEDOM TO EXPLOIT MY NEIGHBOUR (verses 13b, 15)

Verse 13 ends: *but through love be servants of one another.* Christian freedom is no more freedom to do as I please irrespective of the good of my neighbour than it is freedom to do as I please in the indulgence of my flesh. It is freedom to approach God without fear, not freedom to exploit my neighbour without love.

Indeed, so far from having liberty to ignore, neglect or abuse our fellow men, we are commanded to love them, and through love to serve them. We are not to use them as if they were *things* to serve us; we are to respect them as *persons* and give ourselves to serve them. We are even through love to become each other's 'slaves' (the Greek is *douleuete*), 'not to be one master with a lot of slaves, but each to be one poor slave with a lot of masters'[1], sacrificing our

[1] Neill, p. 60.

good for theirs, not theirs to ours. Christian liberty is service not selfishness.

It is a remarkable paradox. For from one point of view Christian freedom is a form of slavery,—not slavery to our flesh, but to our neighbour. We are free in relation to God, but slaves in relation to to each other.

This is the meaning of love. If we love one another we shall serve one another, and if we serve one another we shall not 'bite and devour one another' (verse 15) in malicious talk or action. For biting and devouring are destructive, 'conduct more fitting to wild animals than to brothers in Christ',[1] while love is constructive; it serves. And Paul goes on later (verse 22) to describe some of the marks of love, namely 'patience', 'kindness', 'goodness' and 'faithfulness'. Love is patient towards those who aggravate and provoke us. Love thinks kind thoughts and performs good deeds. Love is faithful, dependable, reliable, trustworthy. Further, if we love one another, we shall 'bear one another's burdens' (6:2). For love is never greedy, never grasping. It is always expansive, never possessive. Truly to love somebody is not to possess him for myself but to serve him for himself.

3. CHRISTIAN FREEDOM IS NOT FREEDOM TO DISREGARD THE LAW (verse 14)

For the whole law is fulfilled in one word, 'You shall love your neighbour as yourself.' We must notice carefully what the apostle writes. He does not say, as some of the 'new moralists' are saying, that if we love one another we can safely *break* the law in the interests of love, but that if we love one another we shall *fulfil* the law, because the whole law is summed up in this one command, 'You shall love your neighbour as yourself.'

What is the Christian's relation to the law? The so-called 'new morality' forces the question upon us with some urgency. It is quite true that Paul says to us, if we are Christians, that we have been set free from the law, that we are no longer under the law and that we must not submit again to the 'yoke of slavery' which is the law (verse 1). But we must take pains to grasp what he means by these expressions. Our Christian freedom from the law which he

[1] Cole, p. 157.

emphasizes concerns our relationship to God. It means that our acceptance depends not on our obedience to the law's demands, but on faith in Jesus Christ who bore the curse of the law when He died. It certainly does not mean that we are free to disregard or disobey the law.

On the contrary, although we cannot gain acceptance by keeping the law, yet once we have been accepted we shall keep the law out of love for Him who has accepted us and has given us His Spirit to enable us to keep it. In New Testament terminology, although our justification depends not on the law but on Christ crucified, yet our sanctification consists in the fulfilment of the law. *Cf.* Romans 8:3, 4.

Moreover, if we love one another as well as God, we shall find that we do obey His law because the whole law of God—at least the second table of the law touching our duty to our neighbour—is fulfilled in this one point: 'You shall love your neighbour as yourself', and murder, adultery, stealing, covetousness and false witness are all infringements of this law of love. Paul says the same thing in 6:2: 'Bear one another's burdens, and so fulfil the law of Christ.'

CONCLUSION

This paragraph speaks relevantly to the contemporary situation in the world and the church, especially regarding the fashionable 'new morality' and the modern rejection of authority. It is concerned with the relationship between liberty, licence, law and love.

It tells us at the outset that we are 'called to freedom', the freedom which is peace with God, the cleansing of our guilty conscience through faith in Christ crucified, the unutterable joy of forgiveness, acceptance, access and sonship, the experience of mercy without merit.

It goes on to describe how this liberty from systems of merit expresses itself in our duty to ourselves, our neighbour and our God. It is freedom not to indulge the flesh, but to control the flesh; freedom not to exploit our neighbour, but to serve our neighbour; freedom not to disregard the law, but to fulfil the law. Everyone who has been truly set free by Jesus Christ expresses his liberty in these three ways, first in self-control, next in loving service of his neighbour, and thirdly in obedience to the law of his God.

This is the freedom with which 'Christ has set us free' (verse 1) and to which we 'were called' (verse 13). We are to stand firm in it, neither relapsing into slavery on the one hand, nor falling into licence on the other.

5:16–25

THE FLESH AND THE SPIRIT

BUT I say, walk by the Spirit, and do not gratify the desires of the flesh. [17] *For the desires of the flesh are against the Spirit, and the desires of the Spirit are against the flesh; for these are opposed to each other, to prevent you from doing what you would.* [18] *But if you are led by the Spirit you are not under the law.* [19] *Now the works of the flesh are plain: immorality, impurity, licentiousness,* [20] *idolatry, sorcery, enmity, strife, jealousy, anger, selfishness, dissension, party spirit,* [21] *envy, drunkenness, carousing, and the like. I warn you, as I warned you before, that those who do such things shall not inherit the kingdom of God.* [22] *But the fruit of the Spirit is love, joy, peace, patience, kindness, goodness, faithfulness,* [23] *gentleness, self-control; against such there is no law.* [24] *And those who belong to Christ Jesus have crucified the flesh with its passions and desires.*

[25] *If we live by the Spirit, let us also walk by the Spirit.*

THE main emphasis of the second half of the Epistle to the Galatians is that in Christ life is liberty. We were in bondage under the curse or condemnation of law, but Christ has set us free from it. We were slaves of sin, but now we are God's children.

Yet each time Paul writes of liberty he adds a warning that it can very easily be lost. Some relapse from liberty into bondage (5:1); others turn their liberty into licence (5:13). This was Paul's theme in the last two paragraphs which we have considered. In particular, in verses 13–15, he has emphasized that true Christian liberty expresses itself in self-control, loving service of our neighbour and obedience to the law of God. The question now is, how are these things possible? And the answer is, by the Holy Spirit. He alone can keep us truly free.

This section in which Paul elaborates this theme is simply full of the Holy Spirit. He is mentioned seven times by name. He is presented as our Sanctifier who alone can oppose and subdue our flesh (verses 16, 17), enable us to fulfil the law so that we are delivered from its harsh dominion (verse 18) and cause the fruit of righteousness to grow in our lives (verses 22, 23). So the enjoyment of Christian liberty depends on the Holy Spirit. True, it is Christ who sets us free. But without the continuing, directing, sanctifying work of the Holy Spirit our liberty is bound to degenerate into licence.

The theme of this paragraph may be divided into two and entitled 'the fact of Christian conflict' and 'the way of Christian victory'.

1. THE FACT OF CHRISTIAN CONFLICT (verses 16–23)

The combatants in the Christian conflict are called 'the flesh' and 'the Spirit'. Verses 16, 17: *Walk by the Spirit, and do not gratify* (NEB 'you will not fulfil') *the desires of the flesh. For the desires of the flesh are against the Spirit, and the desires of the Spirit are against the flesh. . . .* By 'the flesh' Paul means what we are by nature and inheritance, our fallen condition, what the New English Bible and J. B. Phillips call our 'lower nature'. By 'the Spirit' he seems to mean the Holy Spirit Himself who renews and regenerates us, first giving us a new nature and then remaining to dwell in us. More simply, we may say that 'the flesh' stands for what we are by natural birth, 'the Spirit' what we become by new birth, the birth of the Spirit. And these two, the flesh and the Spirit, are in sharp opposition to each other.

Some teachers maintain that the Christian has no inner conflict, no civil war within himself, because (they say) his flesh has been eradicated and his old nature is dead. This passage contradicts such a view. Christian people, in Luther's graphic expression, are 'not stocks and stones', that is, people who 'are never moved with anything, never feel any lust or desires of the flesh'.[1] Certainly, as we learn to walk in the Spirit, the flesh becomes increasingly subdued. But the flesh and the Spirit remain, and the conflict between them is fierce and unremitting. Indeed, one may go further and say that this is a specifically Christian conflict. We do not deny that there is such a thing as moral conflict in non-Christian people, but we assert that it is fiercer in Christians because they possess two natures—flesh and Spirit—in irreconcilable antagonism.

We must consider now the kind of behaviour to which the two natures are prone.

[1] Luther, p. 508.

a. The works of the flesh (verses 19–21)

Now the works of the flesh, Paul says, *are plain*. They are obvious to all. The flesh itself, our old nature, is secret and invisible, but its works, the words and deeds in which it erupts, are public and evident. What are they?

Before looking at his list of 'the works of the flesh', something further needs to be said about the expression 'the lust of the flesh' (verse 16, AV). It is unfortunate that this has come to have a connotation in English which its Greek equivalent did not have. Nowadays 'lust' means 'unrestrained sexual desire' and 'flesh' means 'body', so that 'the lusts of the flesh' and 'the sins of the flesh' are (in common parlance) those connected with our bodily appetites. But Paul's meaning is much wider than this. For him 'the lusts of the flesh' are all the sinful desires of our fallen nature. His ugly catalogue of 'the works of the flesh' puts this beyond question.

This is not to say that his list is exhaustive, for he ends it by saying 'and the like' (verse 21). But those he includes seem to belong to at least four realms—sex, religion, society and drink.

First, the realm of sex: *immorality*, *impurity*, *licentiousness* (verse 19). The word for 'immorality' is normally translated 'fornication' (so AV, NEB), meaning sexual intercourse between unmarried people, but may refer to any kind of unlawful sexual behaviour. Perhaps 'impurity' should be rendered by 'unnatural vice'[1] and 'licentiousness' by 'indecency' (NEB), alluding to 'an open and reckless contempt of propriety'.[2] These three words are sufficient to show that all sexual offences, whether public or private, whether between the married or the unmarried, whether 'natural' or 'unnatural', are to be classed as works of the flesh.

Secondly, the realm of religion: *idolatry*, *sorcery* (verse 20). It is important to see that idolatry is as much a work of the flesh as immorality, and that thus the works of the flesh include offences against God as well as against our neighbour or ourselves. If 'idolatry' is the brazen worship of other gods, 'sorcery' is 'the secret tampering with the powers of evil'.[3]

Thirdly, the realm of society. Paul now gives us eight examples of the breakdown of personal relationships, which the New English Bible translates 'quarrels, a contentious temper, envy, fits of rage,

[1] Cole, p. 161. [2] Lightfoot, p. 210. [3] Lightfoot, p. 211.

selfish ambitions (or 'temper tantrums' and 'canvassing for office'[1]), dissensions, party intrigues, and jealousies' (verses 20, 21).

Fourthly, the realm of drink: *drunkenness, carousing* (or NEB 'drinking bouts orgies', verse 21).

To this list of the works of the flesh in the realms of sex, religion, society and drink, Paul now adds a solemn warning: *I warn you*, he writes, *as I warned you before* (when he was with them in Galatia), *that those who do such things* (the verb *prassontes* referring to habitual practice rather than an isolated lapse) *shall not inherit the kingdom of God* (verse 21). Since God's kingdom is a kingdom of godliness, righteousness and self-control, those who indulge in the works of the flesh will be excluded from it. For such works give evidence that they are not in Christ. And if they are not in Christ, then they are not Abraham's seed, nor 'heirs according to promise' (3:29). For other references to our inheritance in Christ, expected or forfeited, see Galatians 4:7, 30.

b. The fruit of the Spirit (verses 22, 23)

Here we have a cluster of nine Christian graces which seem to portray a Christian's attitude to God, to other people and to himself.

Love, joy, peace. This is a triad of general Christian virtues. Yet they seem primarily to concern our attitude towards God, for a Christian's first love is his love for God, his chief joy is his joy in God and his deepest peace is his peace with God.

Next, *patience, kindness, goodness.* These are social virtues, manward rather than Godward in their direction. 'Patience' is longsuffering towards those who aggravate or persecute. 'Kindness' is a question of disposition, and 'goodness' of words and deeds.

The third triad is *faithfulness, gentleness, self-control.* 'Faithfulness' (AV 'faith') appears to describe the reliability of a Christian man. 'Gentleness' is that humble meekness which Christ exhibited (Mt. 11:29; 2 Cor. 10:1). And both are aspects of the 'self-mastery', or 'self-control', which concludes the list.

So we may say that the primary direction of 'love, joy, peace' is Godward, of 'patience, kindness, goodness' manward, and of 'faithfulness, gentleness and self-control' selfward. And all these are 'the fruit of the Spirit', the natural produce that appears in the lives of

[1] Cole, pp. 161, 163.

Spirit-led Christians. No wonder Paul adds again: *against such there is no law* (verse 23). For the function of law is to curb, to restrain, to deter, and no deterrent is needed here.

Having examined 'the works of the flesh' and 'the fruit of the Spirit' separately, it should be even clearer to us than before that 'the flesh' and 'the Spirit' are in active conflict with one another. They are pulling in opposite directions. There exists between the two 'an interminable, deadly feud'.[1] And the result of this conflict is: 'so that what you will to do you cannot do' (end of verse 17, NEB). The parallel between this little phrase and the second part of Romans 7 is, in my judgment, too close to be accidental. Every renewed Christian can say 'I delight in the law of God, in my inmost self' (Rom. 7:22). That is, 'I love it and long to do it. My new nature hungers for God, for godliness and for goodness. I want to be good and to do good.' That is the language of every regenerate believer. 'But', he has to add, 'by myself, even with these new desires, I cannot do what I want to do. Why not? Because of sin that dwells within me.' Or, as the apostle expresses it here in Galatians 5, 'because of the strong desires of the flesh which lust against the Spirit'.

This is the Christian conflict—fierce, bitter and unremitting. Moreover, it is a conflict in which *by himself* the Christian simply cannot be victorious. He is obliged to say 'I can will what is right, but I cannot do it' (Rom. 7:18) or, speaking as it were to himself, 'ye cannot do the things that ye would' (Gal. 5: 17, AV).

'Is that the whole story?' some perplexed reader will be asking. 'Is the tragic confession that "I cannot do what I want to do" the last word about a Christian's inner moral conflict? Is this all Christianity offers—an experience of continuous defeat?' Indeed, it is not. If we were left to ourselves, we could not do what we would; instead, we would succumb to the desires of our old nature. But if we 'walk by the Spirit' (verse 16), *then* we shall not gratify the desires of the flesh. We shall still experience them, but we shall not indulge them. On the contrary, we shall bear the fruit of the Spirit.

2. THE WAY OF CHRISTIAN VICTORY (verses 24, 25)

What must we do in order to control the lusts of the flesh and to bear the fruit of the Spirit? The brief answer is this: We must

[1] Lightfoot, p. 209.

maintain towards each the proper Christian attitude. In the apostle's own words, we must 'crucify' the flesh and 'walk by' the Spirit.

a. We must crucify the flesh

The phrase occurs in verse 24: *Those who belong to Christ Jesus have crucified the flesh with its passions and desires.* This verse is frequently misunderstood. Please notice that the 'crucifixion' of the flesh described here is something that is done not *to* us but *by* us. It is we ourselves who are said to 'have crucified the flesh'. Perhaps I can best expose the popular misconception by saying that Galatians 5:24 does not teach the same truth as Galatians 2:20 or Romans 6:6. In those verses we are told that by faith-union with Christ 'we have been crucified with him'. But here it is we who have taken action. We 'have crucified' our old nature. It is not now a 'dying' which we have experienced through union with Christ; it is rather a deliberate 'putting to death'.

What does it mean? Paul borrows the image of crucifixion, of course, from Christ Himself who said: 'If any man would come after me, let him deny himself and take up his cross and follow me' (Mk. 8:34). To 'take up the cross' was our Lord's vivid figure of speech for self-denial. Every follower of Christ is to behave like a condemned criminal and carry his cross to the place of execution. Now Paul takes the metaphor to its logical conclusion. We must not only take up our cross and walk with it, but actually see that the execution takes place. We are actually to take the flesh, our wilful and wayward self, and (metaphorically speaking) nail it to the cross. This is Paul's graphic description of repentance, of turning our back on the old life of selfishness and sin, repudiating it finally and utterly.

The fact that 'crucifixion' is to be the fate of the flesh is very significant. It is always perilous to argue from analogy, but I suggest that the following points, far from being fanciful, belong to the notion of crucifixion and cannot be separated from it.

First, a Christian's rejection of his old nature is to be *pitiless*. Crucifixion in the Graeco-Roman world was not a pleasant form of execution, nor was it administered to nice or refined people; it was reserved for the worst criminals, which is why it was such a shameful thing for Jesus Christ to be crucified. If, therefore, we are to 'crucify' our flesh, it is plain that the flesh is not something respectable to be treated with courtesy and deference, but something so evil that it deserves no better fate than to be crucified.

Secondly, our rejection of the old nature will be *painful.* Crucifixion was a form of execution 'attended with intense pain' (Grimm-Thayer). And which of us does not know the acute pain of inner conflict when 'the fleeting pleasures of sin' (Heb. 11:25) are renounced?

Thirdly, the rejection of our old nature is to be *decisive.* Although death by crucifixion was a lingering death, it was a certain death. Criminals who were nailed to a cross did not survive. John Brown draws out the significance of this fact for us: 'Crucifixion . . . produced death not suddenly but gradually . . . True Christians . . . do not succeed in completely destroying it (that is, the flesh) while here below; but they have fixed it to the cross, and they are determined to keep it there till it expire.'[1] Once a criminal had been nailed to the cross, he was left there to die. Soldiers were placed at the scene of execution to guard the victim. Their duty was to prevent anyone from taking him down from the cross, at least until he was dead. Now 'those who belong to Christ Jesus', Paul says, 'have crucified the flesh with its passions and desires'. The Greek verb is in the aorist tense, indicating that this is something we did decisively at the moment of conversion. When we came to Jesus Christ, we repented. We 'crucified' everything we knew to be wrong. We took our old self-centred nature, with all its sinful passions and desires, and nailed it to the cross. And this repentance of ours was decisive, as decisive as a crucifixion. So, Paul says, if we crucified the flesh, we must leave it there to die. We must renew every day this attitude towards sin of ruthless and uncompromising rejection. In the language of Jesus, as Luke records it, every Christian must 'take up his cross *daily*' (Lk. 9:23).

So widely is this biblical teaching neglected, that it needs to be further enforced. The first great secret of holiness lies in the degree and the decisiveness of our repentance. If besetting sins persistently plague us, it is either because we have never truly repented, or because, having repented, we have not maintained our repentance. It is as if, having nailed our old nature to the cross, we keep wistfully

[1] Brown, p. 309.

returning to the scene of its execution. We begin to fondle it, to caress it, to long for its release, even to try to take it down again from the cross. We need to learn to leave it there. When some jealous, or proud, or malicious, or impure thought invades our mind we must kick it out at once. It is fatal to begin to examine it and consider whether we are going to give in to it or not. We have declared war on it; we are not going to resume negotiations. We have settled the issue for good; we are not going to re-open it. We have crucified the flesh; we are never going to draw the nails.

b. We must walk by the Spirit

We turn now to the attitude which we are to adopt towards the Holy Spirit. This is described in two ways. First, it is to be *led by the Spirit* (verse 18). Secondly, it is to *walk by* (AV 'in') *the Spirit* (verses 16 and 25). In both expressions in the Greek text 'the Spirit' comes first for emphasis, a simple dative is used (there is no preposition, whether 'in' or 'by') and the verb is in the present continuous tense. At the same time there is clearly a distinction between 'being led by the Spirit' and 'walking by the Spirit', for the former expression is passive and the latter active. It is the Spirit who does the leading, but we who do the walking.

First, then, Christians are portrayed as being 'led by the Spirit'. The verb is used of a farmer herding cattle, of a shepherd leading sheep, of soldiers escorting a prisoner to court or prison, and of wind driving a ship. It is used metaphorically of both good and evil spirits—of the evil power of Satan leading men astray (*e.g.* 1 Cor. 12:2; Eph. 2:2), and of the Holy Spirit leading Christ during His temptations in the wilderness (Lk. 4: 1, 2) and leading the sons of God today (Rom. 8:14). As our 'leader' the Holy Spirit takes the initiative. He asserts His desires against those of the flesh (verse 17) and forms within us holy and heavenly desires. He puts this gentle pressure upon us, and we must yield to His direction and control.

And His that gentle voice we hear,
Soft as the breath of even,
That checks each fault, that calms each fear,
And speaks of heaven.

For every virtue we possess,
And every victory won,
And every thought of holiness,
Are His alone.

But it is a great mistake to suppose that our whole duty lies in passive submission to the Spirit's control, as if all we had to do was to surrender to His leading. On the contrary, we are ourselves to 'walk', actively and purposefully, in the right way. And the Holy Spirit is the path we walk in, as well as the guide who shows us the way.

This becomes clear when a careful comparison is made between verses 16 and 25. The English of both verses contains the verb to 'walk', but the Greek words are different. The verb in verse 16 is the ordinary one for walking, but that in verse 25 (*stoicheō*) refers literally to people being 'drawn up in line'. Hence it means to 'walk in line' or 'be in line with'. It is used of believers who by sharing Abraham's faith are said to 'walk in line with' his footsteps or follow his example (Rom. 4:12). Similarly, it describes Christians who 'walk in line with' the position they have so far attained (Phil. 3:16) or the requirements of the law (Acts 21:24) or the truth of the gospel (Gal. 6:16). In each of these cases there is a rule, a standard or a principle, which is being followed. In Galatians 5:25 this 'rule' or 'line' is the Holy Spirit Himself and His will. So to 'walk by the Spirit' is deliberately to walk along the path or according to the line which the Holy Spirit lays down. The Spirit 'leads' us; but we are to 'walk by' Him or according to His rule.

As, therefore, we 'crucify the flesh', repudiating what we know to be wrong, so too we must 'walk by the Spirit', setting ourselves to follow what we know to be right. We reject one path to follow another. We turn from what is evil in order to occupy ourselves with what is good. And if it is vital to be ruthless in turning away from the things of the flesh, it is equally vital to be disciplined in turning towards the things of the Spirit. The Scripture says we are to 'set our minds on the things of the Spirit', to 'seek the things that are above', to 'set our minds on things that are above', to 'think about these things' (*i.e.* whatever is true, honourable, just, pure, lovely and gracious).[1]

[1] Rom. 8:5, 6; Col. 3:1, 2; Phil. 4:8.

This will be seen in our whole way of life—in the leisure occupations we pursue, the books we read and the friendships we make. Above all in what older authors called 'a diligent use of the means of grace', that is, in a disciplined practice of prayer and Scripture meditation, in fellowship with believers who provoke us to love and good works, in keeping the Lord's day as the Lord's day, and in attending public worship and the Lord's Supper. In all these ways we occupy ourselves in spiritual things. It is not enough to yield passively to the Spirit's control; we must also walk actively in the Spirit's way. Only so will the fruit of the Spirit appear.

CONCLUSION

We have seen that the works of the flesh are many and evil, that the fruit of the Spirit is lovely and desirable, that flesh and Spirit are in continuous conflict with each other so that by ourselves we cannot do what we want to do, and that our duty is to crucify the flesh, rejecting its evil ways, and to walk by the Spirit, fostering His good ways.

This victory is within reach of every Christian, for every Christian has 'crucified the flesh' (verse 24) and every Christian 'lives by the Spirit' (verse 25). Our task is to take time each day to remember these truths about ourselves, and to live accordingly. If we have crucified the flesh (which we have), then we must leave it securely nailed to the cross, where it deserves to be; we must not finger the nails. And if we live in the Spirit (which we do), then we must walk by the Spirit. So when the tempter comes with evil insinuations, we must round on him savagely, and say to him: 'I belong to Christ. I have crucified the flesh. It is altogether out of the question that I should even dream of taking it down from the cross.' Again, 'I belong to Christ. The Spirit dwells within me. So I shall set my mind on the things of the Spirit and walk by the Spirit, according to His rule and line, from day to day.'

5:26 – 6:5

RECIPROCAL CHRISTIAN RELATIONSHIPS

LET *us have no self-conceit, no provoking of one another, no envy of one another.*

[1] *Brethren, if a man is overtaken in any trespass, you who are spiritual should restore him in a spirit of gentleness. Look to yourself, lest you too be tempted.* [2] *Bear one another's burdens, and so fulfil the law of Christ.* [3] *For if any one thinks he is something, when he is nothing, he deceives himself.* [4] *But let each one test his own work, and then his reason to boast will be in himself alone and not in his neighbour.* [5] *For each man will have to bear his own load.*

IN Galatians 5:16–25 the apostle Paul has described both the Christian conflict between the flesh and the Spirit, and the way of victory through crucifying the flesh and walking by the Spirit.

Galatians 5:26–6:5 describes one of the practical results of this victory. It concerns our personal relationships, especially with fellow-believers in the congregation. This is plain from the exhortations of verses 25 and 26. Verse 25: *If we live by the Spirit, let us also walk by the Spirit.* Verse 26: *Let us have no self-conceit, no provoking of one another, no envy of one another.* Ephesians 5:18 ff. is similar, where the outcome of the command 'Be filled with the Spirit' includes 'addressing one another' and being 'subject to one another'. Both passages show that the first and great evidence of our walking by the Spirit or being filled with the Spirit is not some private mystical experience of our own, but our practical relationships of love with other people. And since the first fruit of the Spirit is love, this is only logical.

But it is easy to talk about 'love' in an abstract and general way; it is much harder to get down to concrete, particular situations in which we actually demonstrate our love for one another. It is some of these which Paul now unfolds. He tells us how, if we are walking by the Spirit, we shall and shall not behave towards each other.

1. HOW CHRISTIANS SHOULD NOT TREAT EACH OTHER (verse 26)

Let us have no self-conceit (AV 'vainglory'), *no provoking of one another, no envy of one another.* This is a very instructive verse because it shows that our conduct to others is determined by our opinion of ourselves. It is when we have 'self-conceit' that we provoke and envy other people. This word (the Greek adjective *kenodoxos*) denotes somebody who has an opinion of himself which is empty, vain or false. He is cherishing an illusion about himself or is just plain conceited. Now, when we are conceited, our relationships with other people are bound to be poisoned. Indeed, whenever relationships with other people deteriorate, conceit is nearly always the basic cause. According to Paul, when we are conceited, we tend to do one of two things; we either 'provoke' one another or 'envy' one another.

First, we provoke one another. This Greek verb (*prokaleō*) is unique in the New Testament. It means to 'challenge' somebody to a contest. It implies that we are so sure of our superiority that we want to demonstrate it. So we challenge people to dispute it in order to give ourselves a chance to prove it. Secondly, we envy one another, being jealous of one another's gifts or attainments.

What the apostle writes here is entirely true to our own experience. Generally speaking, we adopt towards each other one of these two attitudes. We are motivated by feelings either of inferiority or superiority. If we regard ourselves as superior to other people we challenge them, for we want them to know and feel our superiority. If, on the other hand, we regard them as superior to us, we envy them. In both cases our attitude is due to 'vainglory' or 'conceit', to our having such a fantasy opinion of ourselves that we cannot bear rivals.

Very different is that love which is the fruit of the Spirit, which Christians exhibit when they are walking by the Spirit. Such people have no self-conceit, or rather are continuously seeking by the Spirit to subdue it. They do not think of themselves more highly than they ought to think; they think soberly (Rom. 12:3). The Holy Spirit has opened their eyes to see both their own sin and unworthiness and also the importance and value of other people in the sight of God. People with such love regard others as 'more important' and seek every opportunity to serve them.[1]

To sum up, then, truly Christian relationships are governed not by rivalry but by service. The correct attitude to other people is not 'I'm better than you and I'll prove it', nor 'You're better than I and I resent it', but 'You are a person of importance in your own right (because God made you in His own image and Christ died for you) and it is my joy and privilege to serve you'.

2. HOW CHRISTIANS SHOULD TREAT EACH OTHER (verses 2–5)

The general principle is supplied in Galatians 6:2: *Bear one another's burdens, and so fulfil the law of Christ.*

Notice the assumption which lies behind this command, namely that we all have burdens and that God does not mean us to carry them alone. Some people try to. They think it a sign of fortitude not to bother other people with their burdens. Such fortitude is certainly brave. But it is more stoical than Christian. Others remind us that we are told in Psalm 55:22 to 'cast your burden on the Lord, and he will sustain you', and that the Lord Jesus invited the heavy-laden to come to Him and promised to give them rest (Mt. 11:28). They therefore argue that we have a divine burden-bearer who is quite adequate, and that it is a sign of weakness to require any human help. This too is a grievous mistake. True, Jesus Christ alone can bear the burden of our sin and guilt; He bore it in His own body when He died on the cross. But this is not so with our other burdens —our worries, temptations, doubts and sorrows. Certainly, we can cast these burdens on the Lord as well. We can cast *all* our care on Him, since He cares for us (1 Pet. 5:7, AV). But remember that one of the ways in which He bears these burdens of ours is through human friendship.

A striking example of this principle is given us in the career of

[1] Phil. 2:3: 'Do nothing from selfishness or conceit, but in humility count others better than yourselves.' This cannot be a command to regard everybody, including the worst offenders, as morally 'better' (since humility is neither blind nor perverse), but rather to regard them as 'more important' and therefore worthy to be served.

the apostle Paul. At one stage in his life he was terribly burdened. He was worried to death over the Corinthian church and in particular about their reaction to a rather severe letter which he had written to them. His mind could not rest, so great was his suspense. 'We were afflicted at every turn', he wrote, '—fighting without and fear within.' Then he continued: 'But God, who comforts the downcast, comforted us by the coming of Titus' (2 Cor. 7:5, 6). God's comfort was not given to Paul through his private prayer and waiting upon the Lord, but through the companionship of a friend and through the good news which he brought.

Human friendship, in which we bear one another's burdens, is part of the purpose of God for His people. So we should not keep our burdens to ourselves, but rather seek a Christian friend who will help to bear them with us.

By such burden-bearing we 'fulfil the law of Christ' (verse 2). Because of the interesting link in this sentence between 'burdens' and the 'law', it is possible that Paul is casting a side-glance at the Judaizers. Certainly some of the law's requirements are referred to as a burden in the New Testament (*e.g.* Lk. 11:46; Acts 15:10, 28), and the Judaizers were seeking to burden the Galatians with the observance of the law for their acceptance with God. So Paul may be saying to them, in effect, that instead of imposing the law as a burden upon others, they should rather lift their burdens and so fulfil Christ's law.

The 'law of Christ' is to love one another as He loves us; that was the new commandment which He gave (Jn. 13:34; 15:12). So, as Paul has already stated in Galatians 5:14, to love our neighbour is to fulfil the law. It is very impressive that to 'love our neighbour', 'bear one another's burdens' and 'fulfil the law' are three equivalent expressions. It shows that to love one another as Christ loved us may lead us not to some heroic, spectacular deed of self-sacrifice, but to the much more mundane and unspectacular ministry of burden-bearing. When we see a woman, or a child, or an elderly person carrying a heavy case, do we not offer to carry it for them? So when we see somebody with a heavy burden on his heart or mind, we must be ready to get alongside him and share his burden. Similarly, we must be humble enough to let others share ours.

To be a burden-bearer is a great ministry. It is something that every Christian should and can do. It is a natural consequence of walking by the Spirit. It fulfils the law of Christ. 'Therefore', wrote Martin Luther, 'Christians must have strong shoulders and mighty bones'[1]—sturdy enough, that is, to carry heavy burdens.

The apostle continues in verse 3: *For if any one thinks he is something, when he is nothing, he deceives himself.* The implication seems to be that if we do not or will not bear one another's burdens, it is because we think we are above it. We would not demean ourselves to such a thing; it would be beneath our dignity. Again it is apparent, as in Galatians 5:26, that our conduct to *others* is governed by our opinion of *ourselves*. As we provoke and envy other people when we have self-conceit, so when we think we are 'something' we decline to bear their burdens.

But to think thus of ourselves is to be self-deceived. As we saw earlier, conceit is 'vainglory', entertaining a false opinion of ourselves. The truth is that we are not 'something'; we are 'nothing'. Is this an exaggeration? Not when the Holy Spirit has opened our eyes to see ourselves as we are, rebels against the God who made us in His image, deserving nothing at His hand but destruction. When we realize and remember this, we shall not compare ourselves favourably with other people, nor shall we decline to serve them or bear their burdens.

Moreover, when we are Christians, redeemed by God through Jesus Christ, we shall still not compare ourselves with others. It is these comparisons which are so odious and dangerous, as the apostle goes on to say. Verses 4 and 5: *But let each one test his own work, and then his reason to boast will be in himself alone and not in his neighbour. For each man will have to bear his own load.* In other words, instead of scrutinizing our neighbour and comparing ourselves with him, we are to test our 'own work' for we will have to bear 'our own load'. That is, we are responsible to God for our work and must give an account of it to Him one day.

There is no contradiction here between verse 2, 'Bear one another's burdens', and verse 5, 'each man will have to bear his own load'. The Greek word for burden is different, *baros* (verse 2) meaning a weight or heavy load and *phortion* (verse 5) being 'a common term for a man's pack'.[2] So we are to bear one another's 'burdens' which are too heavy for a man to bear alone, but there is one burden which we cannot share—indeed do not need to because

[1] Luther, p. 540. [2] Lightfoot, p. 217.

it is a pack light enough for every man to carry himself—and that is our responsibility to God on the day of judgment. On that day you cannot carry my pack and I cannot carry yours. 'Each man will have to bear his own load.'

3. AN EXAMPLE OF BURDEN-BEARING (verse 1)

In verse 1 the apostle Paul gives his readers a particular example of burden-bearing: *Brethren, if a man is overtaken in any trespass, you who are spiritual should restore him in a spirit of gentleness. Look to yourself, lest you too be tempted.* To 'overtake' somebody in the act of sinning is a not infrequent occurrence. The best-known instance in the New Testament is the woman whom the Pharisees brought to Jesus and described to Him as having been 'caught in the very act of adultery' (Jn. 8:4, NEB). But we have many other, less sensational experiences when somebody has been surprised or detected in a sin. The apostle gives instructions for such a situation. He tells us first what to do, secondly who is to do it, and thirdly how it is to be done.

a. What to do

If a man is overtaken in any trespass, . . . restore him . . . The verb is instructive. *Katartizō* means to 'put in order' and so to 'restore to its former condition' (Arndt-Gingrich). It was used in secular Greek as a medical term for setting a fractured or dislocated bone. It is applied in Mark 1:19 to the apostles who were 'mending' their nets, although Arndt-Gingrich suggest a wider interpretation, namely that after a night's fishing, they were 'overhauling' (NEB) their nets 'by cleaning, mending and folding (them) together'.

Notice how positive Paul's instruction is. If we detect somebody doing something wrong, we are not to stand by doing nothing on the pretext that it is none of our business and we have no wish to be involved. Nor are we to despise or condemn him in our hearts and, if he suffers for his misdemeanour, say 'Serves him right' or 'Let him stew in his own juice'. Nor are we to report him to the minister, or gossip about him to our friends in the congregation. No, we are to 'restore' him, to 'set him back on the right path' (JBP). This is how Luther applies the command: 'run unto him, and reaching out your hand, raise him up again, comfort him with sweet words, and embrace him with motherly arms.'[1]

We are not told here precisely how we are to restore our fallen brother, but we can learn this from the more detailed instructions of Jesus in Matthew 18:15–17. We are to go to our brother and tell him his fault, face to face and privately. Jesus also made our object positive and constructive. We are to seek to 'gain' him, He said, as Paul here says we are to 'restore' him.

b. Who is to do it

You who are spiritual should restore him. Some commentators have thought that Paul is here being sarcastic. They have conjectured that there was a group of super-spiritual people in Galatia who were calling themselves the 'spiritual' party. But there is no evidence that such a party existed and no need to see sarcasm in Paul's words. He is referring to 'mature' or 'spiritual' Christians, whom he is later to describe more fully in 1 Corinthians 2:14–3:4, and whom he has already begun to portray in Galatians 5:16–25. All Christians are indwelt by the Spirit, but 'spiritual' Christians are also 'led by the Spirit' and 'walk by the Spirit', so that 'the fruit of the Spirit' appears in their lives. Indeed, this loving ministry of restoring an erring brother is exactly the kind of thing that we shall do when we are walking by the Spirit. It is only the 'spiritual' Christian who should attempt to restore him.

We may not, however, seize upon this as an excuse to evade an unpalatable task. We may not say 'that excuses me; I'm not spiritual'. Verse 1 is certainly an admission that not all Christians are in fact 'spiritual' Christians, but then all Christians should be, and as such have a responsibility to restore a sinning brother.

c. How it should be done

You who are spiritual should restore him in a spirit of gentleness. Look to yourself, lest you too be tempted. The same Greek word for 'gentleness' (*praotēs*) has occurred in 5:23 as part of the fruit of the Spirit, for 'gentleness', writes Bishop Lightfoot, 'is a characteristic of true spirituality'.[2] One of the reasons why only spiritual Christians should

[1] Luther, p. 538. [2] Lightfoot, p. 216.

attempt the ministry of restoration is that only the spiritual are gentle. Paul then adds that we are ourselves to be watchful, lest we also are tempted. This suggests that gentleness is born of a sense of our own weakness and proneness to sin. J. B. Phillips paraphrases: 'Not with any feeling of superiority but being yourselves on guard against temptation.'

We have seen, then, that when a Christian brother is overtaken in sin, he is to be restored, and that mature, spiritual believers are to exercise this delicate ministry gently and humbly. It is sad that in the contemporary church this plain command of the apostle is more honoured in the breach than the observance. Yet if we walked by the Spirit we would love one another more, and if we loved one another more we would bear one another's burdens, and if we bore one another's burdens we would not shrink from seeking to restore a brother who has fallen into sin. Further, if we obeyed this apostolic instruction as we should, much unkind gossip would be avoided, more serious backsliding prevented, the good of the church advanced, and the name of Christ glorified.

CONCLUSION

We come back to where we started. Those who walk by the Spirit are led into harmonious relationships with one another. Indeed, this reciprocal 'one another' is the word which gives cohesion to the paragraph we have been studying. There is to be 'no provoking of one another' and 'no envy of one another' (5:26), but rather are we to 'bear one another's burdens' (6:2). And this active Christian 'one-anotherness' is an inevitable expression of Christian brotherhood. It is not an accident that Paul addresses his readers as 'brethren' (verse 1). In the Greek the first word and the last word of Galatians 6, apart from the final 'Amen', is the word 'brethren'. Bishop Lightfoot quotes the old Latin commentator Bengel: 'a whole argument lies hidden under this one word.'[1]

Just as the apostle argues about our Christian liberty from the fact that we are God's 'sons', so he argues for responsible Christian conduct from the fact that we are 'brothers'. This paragraph is the New Testament answer to Cain's irresponsible question 'Am I my brother's keeper?' (Gn. 4:9). If a man is my brother, then I am his

[1] Lightfoot, p. 215.

keeper. I am to care for him in love, to be concerned for his welfare. I am neither to assert my fancied superiority over him and 'provoke him', nor resent his superiority over me and 'envy' him. I am to love him and to serve him. If he is heavy-laden, I am to bear his burdens. If he falls into sin, I am to restore him, and that gently. It is to such practical Christian living, brotherly care and service that walking by the Spirit will lead us, and it is by such too that the law of Christ is fulfilled.

6:6–10

SOWING AND REAPING

LET *him who is taught the word share all good things with him who teaches.* [7] *Do not be deceived: God is not mocked, for whatever a man sows, that he will also reap.* [8] *For he who sows to his own flesh will from the flesh reap corruption; but he who sows to the Spirit will from the Spirit reap eternal life.* [9] *And let us not grow weary in well-doing, for in due season we shall reap, if we do not lose heart.* [10] *So then, as we have opportunity, let us do good to all men, and especially to those who are of the household of faith.*

THE apostle Paul is nearing the end of his letter. His main themes have by now been expounded. All he has left are a few final admonitions. At first sight, these instructions and exhortations appear to be very loosely connected, even totally disconnected. But a closer look at them reveals the connecting link. It is the great principle of sowing and reaping. This is stated in epigrammatic form in verse 7: *Whatever a man sows, that he will also reap.* This is a principle of order and consistency which is written into all life, material and moral.

Take agriculture. God promised Noah after the flood that, so long as the earth remained, 'seedtime and harvest', that is, sowing and reaping, would not cease (Gn. 8:22). If a farmer wants a harvest, he must sow his seed in his field; otherwise, there will be no harvest. Moreover, the kind of harvest he will get is determined in advance by the kind of seed he sows. This is true of its nature, its quality and its quantity. If he sows barley seed he will get a barley crop; if he sows wheat seed he will get a wheat crop. Similarly, good seed will produce a good crop, and bad seed a bad crop. Again, if he sows plentifully, he can expect a plentiful harvest, but if he sows sparingly, then he will reap sparingly as well (*cf.* 2 Cor. 9:6). Putting the three together, we may say that if a farmer wants a bumper harvest of a particular corn, then he must not only sow the right seed, but good seed and that plentifully. Only if he does this can he expect a good crop.

Precisely the same principle operates in the moral and spiritual sphere. *Whatever a man sows, that he will also reap.* It is not the reapers who decide what the harvest is going to be like, but the sowers. If a man is faithful and conscientious in his sowing, then he can confidently expect a good harvest. If he 'sows wild oats', as we sometimes say, then he must not expect to reap strawberries! On the contrary, 'those who plough iniquity and sow trouble reap the same' (Jb. 4:8). Or, as Hosea warned his contemporaries (8:7), 'they sow the wind, and they shall reap the whirlwind' (*sc.* of divine judgment).

This principle is an immutable law of God. In order to emphasize it, the apostle prefaces it with both a command ('do not be deceived') and a statement ('God is not mocked').

The possibility of being deceived is mentioned several times in the New Testament. Jesus said that the devil was a liar and the father of lies, and He cautioned His disciples against being led astray.[1] John warns us in his Second Epistle that 'many deceivers have gone out into the world'.[2] Paul begs us in his Letter to the Ephesians: 'Let no one deceive you with empty words.'[3] Already in Galatians he has asked 'who has bewitched' his readers (3:1) and spoken of the person who 'deceives himself' (6:3).

Many people are deceived concerning this inexorable law of seed-time and harvest. They sow their seeds thoughtlessly, nonchalantly, and blind themselves to the fact that the seeds they sow will inevitably produce a corresponding harvest. Or they sow seed of one kind and expect to reap a harvest of another. They imagine that somehow they can get away with it. But this is impossible. So Paul adds: *God is not mocked.* The Greek verb here (*muktērizō*) is striking. It is derived from the word for a nose and means literally to 'turn up the nose at' somebody and so to 'sneer at' or 'treat with contempt'. From this it can signify to 'fool' (NEB) or to 'outwit' (Arndt-Gingrich). What the apostle is saying is that men may fool themselves, but they cannot fool God. They may think that they can escape this law of seed-time and harvest, but they cannot. They may go on sowing their

[1] Jn. 8:44; Mk. 13:5, 6, 22.
[2] 2 Jn. 7. *Cf.* 1 Jn. 2:18–27; 4:1–6.
[3] Eph. 5:6. *Cf.* 1 Cor. 6:9; 2 Thes. 2:3.

seeds and closing their eyes to the consequences, but one day God Himself will bring in the harvest.

From the principle we turn to the application. There are three spheres of Christian experience in which Paul sees the principle operating.

1. CHRISTIAN MINISTRY (verse 6)

Let him who is taught the word share all good things with him who teaches. The Greek word for 'him who is taught the word' is *ho katēchoumenos*, the catechumen, a person who 'is under instruction in the faith' (NEB). This is how Luke describes Theophilus in the Preface to his Gospel (1:4).

Whether the instruction given is private, or in a catechetical school in which converts are being prepared for baptism, or to a whole congregation by their pastor, the principle is the same, that he who is taught the word should help to support his teacher. So a minister may expect to be supported by the congregation. He sows the good seed of God's Word, and he reaps a livelihood.

Some people find this embarrassing. But the biblical principle is emphasized many times. The Lord Jesus said to the Seventy whom He sent out, 'The labourer deserves his wages' (Lk. 10:7). And Paul makes explicit use of the sowing and reaping metaphor to teach the same truth: 'If we have sown spiritual good among you, is it too much if we reap your material benefits?' (1 Cor. 9:11).

If the principle is properly applied, it contains its own safeguards. Nevertheless, we ought to consider its two possible abuses.

a. Abuse by the minister

Luther saw in his own day the danger of obeying this apostolic injunction too readily, for the Roman Catholic church was very wealthy as the people poured money into it, and 'by this excessive liberality of men, the covetousness of the clergy did increase'.[1] Similarly today, although few ministers could be described as overpaid, the popular image of the Christian minister (at least in the western world) seems to be that his job is both 'cushy' and secure. In modern slang, he is 'on to a good thing'. And there is some truth

[1] Luther, p. 547.

in this. Some Christian ministers are tempted to laziness, and some succumb to the temptation. In England ministers are classified as 'self-employed'. Nobody exactly supervises their work. So it is not unknown for ministers to grow slack. It is understandable, therefore, that Paul, although asserting the Lord's command that 'those who proclaim the gospel should get their living by the gospel' (1 Cor. 9:14), nevertheless renounced his own right and preached the gospel free of any charge, earning his living as a tent-maker. Perhaps more of us should endeavour to do the same today in order to correct the impression that ministers are only 'in it for what they can get out of it'. And yet the scriptural principle is clear, that the minister should be set free from secular wage-earning in order to devote himself to the study and the ministry of the Word, and to the care of the flock committed to his charge. As Luther put it, 'it is impossible for one man both to labour day and night to get a living, and at the same time to give himself to the study of sacred learning as the preaching office requireth.'[1]

Is there any safeguard against this possible abuse? I think we may find one in 1 Timothy 5:17: 'Elders who do well as leaders should be reckoned worthy of a double stipend, in particular those who labour at preaching and teaching. For Scripture says, "A threshing ox shall not be muzzled"; and besides, "the workman earns his pay"' (NEB). It is not particularly flattering, perhaps, to find the preacher likened to a threshing ox! But he is also called a 'workman' or labouring man. The Greek word is strong and indicates that he 'toils' at the Word with all his might and main, seeking to understand and apply it. Perhaps preaching is at a low ebb in the church today because we shirk the hard work involved. But if the minister throws himself into his ministry with the energy of a labouring man, and sows good seed in the minds and hearts of the congregation, then he may expect to 'reap' a material livelihood.

b. Abuse by the congregation

If the principle of the congregation paying the minister may encourage the minister to be lazy and neglectful, it may also tempt the congregation to try to control the minister. Some congregations exercise a positive tyranny over their pastor and almost blackmail

[1] Luther, p. 552.

him into preaching what they want to hear. They pay the piper, they say; so they must be allowed to call the tune. And if the minister has a wife and family to support, he is tempted to give way. Of course it is wrong for a minister to yield to such pressure, but it is also wrong for a congregation to put him in this predicament. If the minister sows the good seed of God's Word faithfully, however unpalatable the congregation may find it, he has a right to reap his living. They have no authority to dock his wages because he refuses to dock his words.

The right relationship between teacher and taught, or minister and congregation, is one of *koinōnia*, 'fellowship' or 'partnership'. So Paul writes: 'Let him who is taught the word *share* (*koinōneitō*) all good things with him who teaches.' He shares spiritual things with them, and they share material things with him. Bishop Stephen Neill comments: 'This is not to be regarded as a *payment*. The word "shared" is a rich Christian word, which is used of our *fellowship* in the Holy Spirit.'[1]

2. CHRISTIAN HOLINESS (verse 8)

For he who sows to his own flesh will from the flesh reap corruption; but he who sows to the Spirit will from the Spirit reap eternal life. This is another sphere in which the 'seed-time and harvest' principle operates. Paul moves from the particular to the general, from Christian ministers and their support to Christian people and their moral behaviour. He reverts to the theme of the flesh and the Spirit which he has treated at some length in Galatians 5:16–25. There in Galatians 5 the Christian's life is likened to a battleground, and the flesh and the Spirit are two combatants at war with each other upon it. But here in Galatians 6 the Christian's life is likened to a country estate, and the flesh and the Spirit are two fields in which we may sow seed. Further, the harvest we reap depends on *where* and on *what* we sow.

This is a vitally important and much neglected principle of holiness. We are not the helpless victims of our nature, temperament and environment. On the contrary, what we become depends largely on how we behave; our character is shaped by our conduct. According to Galatians 5 the Christian's duty is to 'walk by the Spirit', according to Galatians 6 to 'sow to the Spirit'. Thus the Holy

[1] Neill, p. 71.

Spirit is likened both to the path along which we walk (Gal. 5) and to the field in which we sow (Gal. 6). How can we expect to reap the *fruit* of the Spirit if we do not sow in the *field* of the Spirit? The old adage is true: 'Sow a thought, reap an act; sow an act, reap a habit; sow a habit, reap a character; sow a character, reap a destiny.' This is good, biblical teaching.

Let us examine the two kinds of sowing which are possible, namely 'sowing to the flesh' and 'sowing to the Spirit'.

a. Sowing to the flesh

We have seen that our 'flesh' is our lower nature 'with its passions and desires' (5:24) which, if unchecked, break out in 'the works of the flesh' (5:19–21). This lower nature is in each of us and remains in us even after conversion and baptism. It is one of the fields of our human estate in which we may sow.

To 'sow to the flesh' is to pander to it, to cosset, cuddle and stroke it, instead of crucifying it. The seeds we sow are largely thoughts and deeds. Every time we allow our mind to harbour a grudge, nurse a grievance, entertain an impure fantasy, or wallow in self-pity, we are sowing to the flesh. Every time we linger in bad company whose insidious influence we know we cannot resist, every time we lie in bed when we ought to be up and praying, every time we read pornographic literature, every time we take a risk which strains our self-control, we are sowing, sowing, sowing to the flesh. Some Christians sow to the flesh every day and wonder why they do not reap holiness. Holiness is a *harvest*; whether we reap it or not depends almost entirely on what and where we sow.

b. Sowing to the Spirit

To 'sow to the Spirit' is the same as 'to set the mind on the Spirit' (Rom. 8:6) and to 'walk by the Spirit' (Gal. 5:16, 25). Again, the seeds we sow are our thoughts and deeds. We are to 'seek' and to 'set our minds on' the things of God, 'things that are above, not . . . things that are on earth' (Col. 3:1, 2; contrast Phil. 3:19). By the books we read, the company we keep and the leisure occupations we pursue we can be 'sowing to the Spirit'. Then we are to foster disciplined habits of devotion in private and in public, in daily prayer and Bible reading, and in worship with the Lord's people on the Lord's Day. All this is 'sowing to the Spirit'; without it there can be no harvest of the Spirit, no 'fruit of the Spirit'.

Paul distinguishes between the two harvests as well as between the two sowings. The results are only logical. If we sow to the flesh, we shall 'from the flesh reap corruption'. That is, a process of moral decay will set in. We shall go from bad to worse until we finally perish. If, on the other hand, we sow to the Spirit, we shall 'from the Spirit reap eternal life'. That is, a process of moral and spiritual growth will begin. Communion with God (which is eternal life) will develop now until in eternity it becomes perfect.

Therefore, if we want to reap a harvest of holiness, our duty is twofold. First, we must avoid sowing to the flesh, and secondly we must keep sowing to the Spirit. We must ruthlessly eliminate the first and concentrate our time and energies on the second. It is another way of saying (as in Gal. 5) that we must 'crucify the flesh' and 'walk by the Spirit'. There is no other way of growing in holiness.

3. CHRISTIAN WELL-DOING (verses 9, 10)

And let us not grow weary in well-doing, for in due season we shall reap, if we do not lose heart. So then, as we have opportunity, let us do good to all men, and especially to those who are of the household of faith. The subject changes somewhat from personal holiness to doing good, helping others, engaging in philanthropic activity in the church or community. But the apostle treats this too under the metaphor of sowing and reaping.

Some incentive is certainly needed in Christian well-doing. Paul recognizes this, for he urges his readers not to 'grow weary' or 'lose heart' (*cf.* 2 Thes. 3:13). Active Christian service is tiring, exacting work. We are tempted to become discouraged, to slack off, even to give up.

So the apostle gives us this incentive: he tells us that doing good is like sowing seed. If we persevere in sowing, then 'in due season we shall reap, if we do not lose heart'. If the farmer tires of sowing and leaves half his field unsown, he will reap only half a crop. It is the same with good deeds. If we want a harvest, then we must finish the sowing and be patient, like the farmer who 'waits for the precious fruit of the earth, being patient over it . . .' (Jas. 5:7). As John Brown put it: 'Christians frequently act like children in reference to this harvest. They would sow and reap in the same day.'[1]

If the sowing is the doing of good works in the community, what is the harvest? Paul does not tell us; he leaves us to guess. But the patient doing of good in the church or community always produces good results. It may bring comfort, relief or assistance to people in need. It may lead a sinner to repentance and so to salvation; Jesus Himself spoke of this work as sowing and reaping (Mt. 9:37; Jn. 4:35–38). It may help to arrest the moral deterioration of society (this is the function of 'the salt of the earth') and even to make it a sweeter and more wholesome place to live in. It may increase men's respect for what is beautiful, good and true, especially in days when standards are slipping fast. And it will bring good to the doer as well—not indeed salvation (for this is a free gift of God), but some reward in heaven for faithful service, which will probably take the form of yet more responsible service.

So then (Paul continues (verse 10), since the sowing of good seed results in a good harvest), *as we have opportunity* (and this earthly life is full of such opportunity), *let us do good to all men, and especially to those who are of the household of faith.* This household consists of our fellow-believers, who share with us 'like precious faith' (2 Pet. 1:1, AV) and so are our brothers and sisters in the family of God. As the old saying goes, 'Charity begins at home', towards kinsmen who may claim our first loyalty, although Christian charity must never stop there. We are to love and serve our enemies, Jesus said, not only our friends. Thus, a 'patient continuance in well-doing' is a characteristic of the true Christian, a characteristic so indispensable that it will be taken as evidence of saving faith on the Judgment Day (see Rom. 2:7, AV).

CONCLUSION

We have considered the three spheres of the Christian life to which Paul applies his inexorable principle that 'whatever a man sows, that he will also reap'. In the first, the seed is *God's Word*, sown by teachers in the minds and hearts of the congregation. In the second, the seed is *our own thoughts and deeds*, sown in the field of the flesh or

[1] Brown, p. 344.

the Spirit. In the third, the seed is *good works*, sown in the lives of other people in the community.

And in each case, although the seed and the soil are different, seed-time is followed by harvest. The teacher who sows God's Word will reap his living; it is God's purpose that he should. The sinner who sows to the flesh will reap corruption. The believer who sows to the Spirit will reap eternal life, an ever-deepening communion with God. The Christian philanthropist who sows good works in the community will reap a good crop in the lives of those he serves and a reward for himself in eternity.

In none of these spheres can God be mocked. In each the same principle invariably operates. And since we cannot fool God, we are fools if we try to fool ourselves! We must neither ignore nor resist this law, but accept it and co-operate with it. We must have the good sense to allow it to govern our lives. 'Whatever a man sows, that he will also reap.' We must expect to reap what we sow. Therefore, if we want to reap a good harvest, we must sow, and keep sowing, good seed. Then, in due time, we shall reap.

6:11-18

THE ESSENCE OF THE CHRISTIAN RELIGION

SEE with what large letters I am writing to you with my own hand. [12] *It is those who want to make a good showing in the flesh that would compel you to be circumcised, and only in order that they may not be persecuted for the cross of Christ.* [13] *For even those who receive circumcision do not themselves keep the law, but they desire to have you circumcised that they may glory in your flesh.* [14] *But far be it from me to glory except in the cross of our Lord Jesus Christ, by which the world has been crucified to me, and I to the world.* [15] *For neither circumcision counts for anything, nor uncircumcision, but a new creation.* [16] *Peace and mercy be upon all who walk by this rule, upon the Israel of God.*

[17] *Henceforth let no man trouble me; for I bear on my body the marks of Jesus.*

[18] *The grace of our Lord Jesus Christ be with your spirit, brethren. Amen.*

PAUL has now reached the end of his letter. So far he has been dictating to an amanuensis, but now, as his custom was, he takes the pen from his secretary's hand, in order to add a personal postscript. Usually this was just to append his signature as a guarantee against forgery (*cf.* 2 Thes. 3:17). Sometimes he would include a final exhortation or the grace. But on this occasion he writes several final sentences in his personal handwriting.

Verse 11: *See with what large letters I am writing to you with my own hand.* Various suggestions have been made about these 'large letters'. Perhaps he is referring to 'the sprawling untidy letters' of an amateur,[1] for he was no professional scribe and was probably more accustomed to write in Hebrew than in Greek. Or perhaps his large letters were due to bad eyesight, to which possibility we have already referred in connection with the 'bodily ailment' of Galatians 4:13-15. But most commentators consider that he used large letters

[1] Cole, p. 180.

deliberately, either because he was treating his readers like children (rebuking their spiritual immaturity by using baby writing) or simply for emphasis, 'to arrest the eye and rivet the mind',[1] much as we would use capital letters or underline words today. Indeed it was a kind of underlining. J. B. Phillips adds a footnote to his paraphrase: 'According to centuries-old Eastern usage, this could easily mean, "Note how heavily I have pressed upon the pen in writing this." Thus it could be translated, "Notice how heavily I underline these words to you."'

What, then, does Paul emphasize? He emphasizes the principal themes of the Christian gospel. Once again he contrasts himself with the Judaizers, and so the two religious systems they represented. As he does so, he pinpoints the vital issues at stake. Reading his words, we are lifted out of the controversy between Paul and the Judaizers in the first century AD and are brought right into the twentieth century. We even catch a glimpse of the course of church history down the ages, in which these issues have been continuously debated. Here are two questions about the essence of the Christian religion.

1. OUTWARD OR INWARD? (verses 12, 13)

Is the essence of the Christian religion outward or inward? We must answer that Christianity is fundamentally not a religion of external ceremonies, but something inward and spiritual, in the heart.

But the Judaizers concentrated on something outward, namely on circumcision. In verses 12 and 13, they are described not only as 'those who receive circumcision' themselves, but as those who 'would compel you to be circumcised' or (NEB) 'are trying to force circumcision upon you'. It is with justice that they are sometimes called 'the circumcision party'. Several times in these pages we have considered their party-cry, 'unless you are circumcised . . . you cannot be saved' (Acts 15:1); they thus denied that salvation was by faith only.

Why did they do this? Paul is very outspoken. Verse 12: they *want to make a good showing in the flesh* or (NEB) 'to make a fair outward

[1] Lightfoot, p. 65.

and bodily show'. Verse 13: ... *that they may glory in your flesh.* Notice the repetition of the word 'flesh'. Circumcision was performed on the body. It is quite true God gave it to Abraham as a sign of His covenant. But in itself it was nothing. Yet the Judaizers were elevating it to an ordinance of central importance, insisting that without it nobody could be saved. But how could an outward and bodily operation secure the salvation of the soul or be an indispensable condition of salvation? It was palpably ridiculous.

Yet the same mistake is made today by those who attach an exaggerated importance to baptism and teach the doctrine of baptismal regeneration. Baptism is important, as circumcision was important. The risen Christ gave baptism to the church, as God gave circumcision to Abraham. Baptism is a sign of covenant membership, as circumcision was. But both baptism and circumcision, however great and spiritual the truths they signify, are themselves outward and bodily acts. And it is absurd to magnify such things as indispensable means of salvation and then to go on to boast about them. It was a kind of obsession with 'ecclesiastical statistics', as Dr. Cole puts it,[1] bragging about 'so many circumcisions in a given year' just as we might brag of so many baptisms or confirmations.

What, then, is of central importance? Verse 15 supplies the answer: *For neither circumcision counts for anything, nor uncircumcision, but a new creation.* What matters primarily is not whether a man has been circumcised (or baptized) or not, but whether he has been born again and is now a new creation. Circumcision was, and baptism is, an outward sign and seal of this. The circumcision of the body symbolized the circumcision of the heart (*cf.* Rom. 2:29). Similarly, baptism with water symbolizes the baptism of the Holy Spirit. And it is a lamentable tragedy when men become so topsy-turvy in their thinking that they substitute the sign for the thing signified, magnify a bodily ceremonial at the expense of a change of heart, and make circumcision or baptism the way of salvation instead of the new creation. Circumcision and baptism are things of the 'flesh', outward and visible ceremonies performed by men; the new creation is a birth of the Spirit, an inward and invisible miracle performed by God.

Throughout history God's people have tended to repeat this same

[1] Cole, p. 181.

mistake. They have debased a religion of the heart into a superficial, outward show, and God has repeatedly sent His messengers to reprove them and to recall them to a spiritual and inward religion. This was the great fault of Israel in the eighth and seventh centuries BC, when God through the prophets complained, 'this people draw near with their mouth and honour me with their lips, while their hearts are far from me' (Is. 29:13). Jesus applied this Scripture to the scribes and Pharisees of His day and exposed their hypocrisy (*e.g.* Mk. 7:6, 7). A similar religious formalism marked the medieval church before the Reformation, and eighteenth-century Anglicanism until Wesley and Whitefield gave us back the gospel. And so much contemporary 'churchianity' is the same—dry, dull, dismal and dead, largely an external show. Indeed, it is natural to fallen man to decline from the real, the inward and the spiritual, and to fabricate a substitute religion which is easy and comfortable because its demands are external and ceremonial only. But outward things matter little in comparison with the new creation or the new birth.

This is not to say that the bodily and the external have no place, for what is in the heart needs to be expressed through the lips, and what is inward and spiritual in religion needs to have some outward expression. But the essence is the inward; outward forms are valueless if inward reality is lacking.

2. HUMAN OR DIVINE? (verses 13–16)

Our second question is whether the essence of the Christian religion is human or divine. In other words, is it fundamentally a matter of what we do for God or of what He has done for us?

In their concentration upon circumcision the Judaizers made a second mistake. For circumcision was not only an outward and bodily ritual; it was also a *human* work, performed by one human being on another. More than that. As a religious symbol, circumcision committed people to keep the law: 'It is necessary', the Judaizers said, 'to circumcise them, and to charge them to keep the law of Moses' (Acts 15:5). They insisted upon obedience to the law because they believed that man's salvation depended upon it. Their idea of the way of salvation was that the death of Christ was insufficient; we still have to merit the favour and forgiveness of God by our own good works. So their religion was a human religion. It began with a human work (circumcision) and continued with more human work (obedience to the law).

Paul challenges this teaching vigorously. He even impugns the motives of the Judaizers and calls their bluff. They cannot seriously believe that salvation is a reward for obedience to the law, he argues, because they 'do not themselves keep the law' (verse 13). So they know that salvation cannot be earned. Why then do they still insist upon meritorious works? Paul's answer is: 'their sole object is to escape persecution for the cross of Christ' (verse 12, NEB). *Cf.* 5:11.

And what is there about the cross of Christ which angers the world and stirs them up to persecute those who preach it? Just this: Christ died on the cross for us sinners, becoming a curse for us (3:13). So the cross tells us some very unpalatable truths about ourselves, namely that we are sinners under the righteous curse of God's law and we cannot save ourselves. Christ bore our sin and curse precisely because we could gain release from them in no other way. If we could have been forgiven by our own good works, by being circumcised and keeping the law, we may be quite sure that there would have been no cross. *Cf.* Galatians 2:21. Every time we look at the cross Christ seems to say to us, 'I am here because of you. It is your sin I am bearing, your curse I am suffering, your debt I am paying, your death I am dying.' Nothing in history or in the universe cuts us down to size like the cross. All of us have inflated views of ourselves, especially in self-righteousness, until we have visited a place called Calvary. It is there, at the foot of the cross, that we shrink to our true size.

And of course men do not like it. They resent the humiliation of seeing themselves as God sees them and as they really are. They prefer their comfortable illusions. So they steer clear of the cross. They construct a Christianity without the cross, which relies for salvation on their works and not on Jesus Christ's. They do not object to Christianity so long as it is not the faith of Christ crucified. But Christ crucified they detest. And if preachers preach Christ crucified, they are opposed, ridiculed, persecuted. Why? Because of the wounds which they inflict on men's pride.

The attitude of the apostle Paul was totally at variance with these views. Verse 14: *But far be it from me to glory except in the cross of our Lord Jesus Christ, by which the world has been crucified to me, and I to the world.* The cross for Paul was not something to escape, but the object of his boasting. The truth is that we cannot boast in ourselves and in the cross simultaneously. If we boast in ourselves and in our ability to save ourselves, we shall never boast in the cross and in the ability of Christ crucified to save us. We have to choose. Only if we have humbled ourselves as hell-deserving sinners shall we give up boasting of ourselves, fly to the cross for salvation and spend the rest of our days glorying in the cross.

As a result, we and the world have parted company. Each has been 'crucified' to the other. 'The world' is the society of unbelievers. Previously we were desperately anxious to be in favour with the world. But now that we have seen ourselves as sinners and Christ crucified as our sin-bearer, we do not care what the world thinks or says of us or does to us. 'The world has been crucified to me, and I to the world.'

So, then, Paul has contrasted false and true religion. On the one hand was circumcision, standing for the outward and the human, a formal external religion and our own efforts to save ourselves. On the other is the cross of Christ and the new creation, the finished work of Christ on the cross to redeem us and the inward work of the Spirit in our hearts to regenerate and sanctify us. These are fundamental parts of the gospel. No-one has understood the gospel who has not grasped that Christianity is first inward and spiritual, and secondly a divine work of grace.

Further, these two principles of the gospel are always and everywhere the same, not only in first-century Galatia, but in the whole church of all time. Verse 16: *Peace and mercy be upon all who walk by this rule, upon the Israel of God.* Here Paul teaches three great truths about the church.

a. The church is the Israel of God

'All who walk by this rule' and 'the Israel of God' are not two groups, but one. The connecting particle *kai* should be translated 'even', not 'and', or be omitted (as in RSV). The Christian church enjoys a direct continuity with God's people in the Old Testament. Those who are in Christ today are 'the true circumcision' (Phil. 3:3), 'Abraham's offspring' (Gal. 3:29) and 'the Israel of God'.

b. The church has a rule to direct it

God's people, God's 'Israel', are said to 'walk by this rule'. The Greek word for 'rule' is *kanōn*, which means a measuring rod or rule, 'the carpenter's or surveyor's line by which a direction is taken'.[1] So the church has a 'rule' by which to direct itself. This is the 'canon' of Scripture, the doctrine of the apostles, and especially in the context of Galatians 6 the cross of Christ and the new creation. Such is the rule by which the church must walk and continuously judge and reform itself.

c. The church enjoys peace and mercy only when it walks by this rule

'Peace and mercy be upon all who walk by this rule, upon the Israel of God.' How can the church be sure of God's mercy and blessing? How can the church experience peace and unity among its own members? The only answer to both questions is 'when it walks by this rule'. Conversely, it is sinful neglect of 'this rule', the apostolic faith of the Bible, which is the main reason why the contemporary church seems to be enjoying so little of the mercy of God and so little internal peace and harmony. 'Peace upon Israel'[2] is impossible when the church departs from its God-given rule.

CONCLUSION (verses 17 and 18)

Verse 17: *Henceforth let no man trouble me; for I bear on my body the marks of Jesus.* The Greek word for 'marks' is *stigmata*. Medieval churchmen believed that these were the scars in the hands, feet and side of Jesus, and that Paul by sympathetic identification with Him found the same scars appearing in his body. It was said that as Francis of Assisi contemplated the wounds of Christ, there appeared in his hands, feet and side 'blackish, fleshy excrescences', exuding a little blood. Some accounts even said that nails like iron had grown out of his flesh, black, hard and fixed. Up to the beginning of the twentieth century no fewer than 321 claims to such 'stigmatization' had been made, in some of which, in addition to the five wounds in hands, feet and side, it was said that marks appeared also on the forehead (where Christ wore the crown of thorns), on the shoulder

[1] Lightfoot, p. 224.
[2] For this phrase *cf.* Nu. 6:24–26; Pss. 125:5; 128:6.

(where He bore the cross) and on the back (where He was scourged), some being accompanied by acute pain and profuse bleeding. Those cases which seem to be well attested would today be termed 'neuropathic bleedings', caused by sub-conscious auto-suggestion. B. B. Warfield gives a full account of claims to stigmatization in his *Miracles, Yesterday and Today*.[1]

It is most unlikely, however, that the *stigmata* of Jesus which Paul bore on his body were of this kind. Doubtless they were rather wounds which he had received while being persecuted for Jesus' sake. According to 2 Corinthians 11:23–25 he had received 'countless beatings'—five times the thirty-nine lashes of the Jews, three times beaten with rods and once stoned. Some of these sufferings may already have been endured before the time of his writing this Epistle. Certainly he had already been stoned in Lystra, one of the Galatian cities, and left in the gutter for dead (Acts 14:19). The wounds which his persecutors had inflicted on him, and the permanent scars they left behind—these were 'the marks of Jesus'.

The word *stigmata* was used in secular Greek for the branding of a slave. It is possible that Paul had this in mind. He was a slave of Jesus; he had received his branding in his persecutions. The word was also employed for 'religious tattooing' (Arndt-Gingrich). Perhaps Paul was claiming that persecution, not circumcision, was the authentic Christian 'tattoo'.

This was the ground of his plea 'henceforth let no man trouble me' or, as J. B. Lightfoot interprets it, 'let no man question my authority'.[2] Paul longed to be left alone by these false teachers. As a Jew he had on his body the mark the Judaizers were emphasizing; but he had other marks too, proving him 'to belong to Jesus Christ, not to Jewry'.[3] He had not avoided persecution for the cross of Christ. On the contrary, he carried wounds on his body which designated him a true slave, a faithful devotee of Jesus Christ.

Finally, verse 18: *The grace of our Lord Jesus Christ be with your spirit, brethren. Amen.* Paul had begun the Epistle with his customary salutation of grace (Gal. 1:3) and gone on to express his astonishment that the Galatians were 'so quickly deserting' the God who had called them 'in the grace of Christ' (1:6). Indeed, the whole

[1] *Miracles, Yesterday and Today*, by B. B. Warfield (Eerdmans, 1953), pp. 84–92.

[2] Lightfoot, p. 225.

[3] Cole, p. 185.

letter is dedicated to the theme of God's grace, His unmerited favour to sinners. So he ends on the same note.

Thus the authentic characteristic of the gospel is 'the grace of our Lord Jesus Christ', and of the gospel preacher 'the marks of Jesus'. This is so for all God's people. Paul bore the marks of Jesus on his body and the grace of Jesus in his spirit. And he desired his readers to have the same, for they were his 'brethren'—the last word of the Epistle—in the family of God.

A REVIEW OF THE EPISTLE

IT may be helpful, in conclusion, if we attempt to review the whole Epistle, or at least to underline its main themes.

We have seen that the background, the situation which called it forth, was the presence in the Galatian churches of certain false teachers. Directly or indirectly Paul alludes to them throughout. They were 'troubling' the church. The same word occurs in Galatians 1:7 and 5:10 and means to 'disturb, unsettle, throw into confusion' (Arndt-Gingrich). And the confusion they were spreading was caused by their erroneous ideas. They were perverting the gospel, and Paul confronts them with hot indignation.

There were three main points at issue between Paul and the Judaizers, and they are still vital issues in the church today. The first is the question of authority: how do we know what and whom to believe or disbelieve? The second is the question of salvation: how can we get right with God, receiving the forgiveness of our sins and being restored to His favour and fellowship? The third is the question of holiness: how can we control the sinful desires of our fallen nature and live a life of righteousness and love? Addressing himself to these questions, Paul devotes approximately the first two chapters of the Epistle to the question of authority, chapters 3 and 4 to the question of salvation, and chapters 5 and 6 to the question of holiness.

1. THE QUESTION OF AUTHORITY

This was the fundamental issue. Paul and Barnabas founded the Galatian churches on their first missionary journey by their preaching and teaching. After their departure other teachers arrived—teachers who claimed to have the authority and backing of the Jerusalem church and who began to undermine the teaching of Paul. As a result, the Galatians were in a dilemma. Here were two sets of teachers, each claiming to bring God's truth, but contradicting one another. Which were the Galatians to listen to and believe? Both seemed to have good credentials. Both were holy, godly, upright and intelligent men, and both were plausible, winsome and dogmatic. Which were they to choose?

The same situation obtains in the church today except that, instead of a simple alternative between two viewpoints, we are faced with a bewildering variety of opinions to choose from. Moreover, each group has its particular appeal; its spokesmen are reputable scholars; and its supporters include theologians and bishops. Each group sounds reasonable and buttresses its case with strong arguments. But they all contradict one another. So how can we know which to choose and whom to follow?

We must see clearly what Paul does in this situation. He asserts his authority as an apostle of Jesus Christ. He expects the Galatians to receive his gospel not just because of *it*, but because of *him*, not because of its superior truth, but because of his superior authority. The authority the Judaizers boasted was an ecclesiastical authority; they claimed to come from and to speak for the Jerusalem church. Paul insists, on the other hand, that both his mission and his message came not from the church but from Christ Himself. This is the argument of Galatians 1 and 2, in which he boldly advances his claim and then supports it by rehearsing the history of his conversion and his subsequent relations with the Jerusalem apostles. It was Christ who authorized him, not they, although, when he did later confer with them, they whole-heartedly endorsed his mission and message.

Conscious of his apostolic authority, Paul expects the Galatians to accept it. They had done this on the first missionary journey, receiving him 'as an angel of God, as Christ Jesus' (4:14). Now that his authority is being challenged and his message contradicted, he still expects them to recognize his authority as Christ's apostle: 'I have confidence in the Lord that you will take no other view than mine' (5:10). The original message, which he had preached to them (1:8) and which they had received (1:9), was to be normative. If anybody preached a gospel contrary to this, however august a personage he might be, 'let him be accursed'.

Almost deafened by the babel of voices in the contemporary church, how are we to decide whom to follow? The answer is the same: we must test them all by the teaching of the apostles of Jesus Christ. 'Peace and mercy' will be on the church when it 'walks by this rule' (6:16). Indeed, this is the only kind of apostolic succession we can accept—not a line of bishops stretching back to the apostles and claiming to be their successors (for the apostles were unique in both authorization and inspiration, and they have no successors), but loyalty to the apostolic doctrine of the New Testament. The teaching of the apostles, now permanently preserved in the New Testament, is to regulate the beliefs and practices of the church of every generation. This is why the Bible is over the church and not *vice versa*. The apostolic authors of the New Testament were commissioned by Christ, not by the church, and wrote with the authority of Christ, not of the church. 'To that authority (*sc*. of the apostles),' as the Anglican bishops said at the 1958 Lambeth Conference, 'the Church must ever bow.' Would that it did! The only church union schemes which can be pleasing to God and beneficial to the church are those which first distinguish between apostolic traditions and ecclesiastical traditions and then subject the latter to the former.

2. THE QUESTION OF SALVATION

How can sinners be 'justified', accepted in the sight of God? How can a holy God forgive sinful men, reconcile them to Himself and restore them to His favour and fellowship?

Paul's answer is straightforward. Salvation is possible only through the atoning death of Jesus Christ on the cross. The Epistle is full of the cross. Paul describes his preaching ministry as 'placarding' Christ crucified before men's eyes (3:1) and his personal philosophy as 'glorying' in the cross alone (6:14). But why was the cross the subject of his preaching and the object of his boasting? What did Christ do on the cross? Consider these three statements in Galatians: He 'gave himself for our sins to deliver us from the present evil age' (1:4); 'the Son of God . . . loved me and gave himself for me' (2:20); and 'Christ redeemed us from the curse of the law, having become a curse for us' (3:13). That is to say, the sense in which He *gave Himself for us* is that He gave Himself *for our sins*, and the sense in which He gave Himself for our sins is that He *became a curse for us*. This phrase can mean only that God's 'curse' (His righteous displeasure and judgment), which rests upon all who break

His law (3:10), was transferred to Christ on the cross. He bore our curse that we might receive the blessing which God had promised to Abraham (3:14).

What, then, must we do to be saved? In a sense, nothing! Jesus Christ has done it all in His curse-bearing death. Our only part is to believe in Jesus, to trust Him without reserve to apply to us personally the benefits of His death. For 'a man is not justified by works of the law but through faith in Jesus Christ' (2:16). The sole function of faith is to unite us to Christ, in whom we receive justification, adoption and the gift of the Spirit.

The Judaizers, on the other hand, were troubling the church by insisting that faith in Jesus was not enough. Circumcision and law-obedience must be added to it. This perversion of the gospel Paul vigorously denies. If people could win salvation by the law, he says, 'then Christ died to no purpose' (2:21). If we contribute our works to the winning of salvation, then we detract from the adequacy of Christ's work. If in His death He bore our sin and curse, then the cross is a sufficient sacrifice for sin and nothing whatever needs to be added to it. Such is 'the stumbling-block of the cross' (5:11), because it tells us that salvation is a gift freely bestowed on the ground of Christ's death and that to it we can contribute precisely nothing.

So the church is 'the household of faith' (6:10). Faith is the chief mark of God's children. We are a family of believers, and faith is the factor which unites us with all God's people of every place and age.

a. Faith unites us with God's people of the past

If we believe, we are the sons of Abraham (3:7, 29), for he was justified by faith (3:6) just as we are. In Christ we inherit Abraham's blessing (3:14). Thus, it is faith which binds together the Old and New Testaments and makes the Bible one book instead of two. As we read the Old Testament authors, we have no difficulty in recognizing them as our fellow-believers.

b. Faith unites us with God's people of the present

Galatians 3:26, 28: 'For in Christ Jesus you are all sons of God, through faith. There is neither Jew nor Greek, there is neither slave nor free, there is neither male nor female; for you are all one in Christ Jesus.' This shows that if we are in Christ by faith we are both 'sons of God' and 'all one'. External distinctions of race, rank and sex are all rendered null and void. So far as our relationship to God is concerned, they count for nothing. It is to be 'in Christ' which matters. And Paul refuses to tolerate any teaching or action which is inconsistent with this. So he castigates the Judaizers for their insistence on circumcision and opposes Peter to his face when he withdraws from table-fellowship with uncircumcised Gentile believers.

Still today faith abolishes distinctions. We have no right to deny our fellowship at the Lord's Table to any Christians who are in Christ by faith, on the ground that they lack episcopal confirmation, total immersion, the right coloured skin, an acceptable culture or anything else. There is a place for order and discipline in each church, to ensure that its members are in Christ by faith. But there is no place for ecclesiastical, social or racial discrimination. The church is 'the household of faith'; it is faith in Christ crucified which levels and unites us.

3. THE QUESTION OF HOLINESS

The Judaizers caricatured Paul's gospel that justification was by grace alone through faith alone; they hinted that in this case good words did not matter and you could evidently live as you please. Paul denies this too. He agrees that Christians are 'free' and urges them to 'stand fast' in the freedom with which Christ has set them free (5:1), but he adds 'only do not use your freedom as an opportunity for the flesh' (5:13). Christian liberty is not licence. Christians have been freed from the bondage of the law in the sense that they have been delivered from the law as a way of salvation. But this does not mean that they are free to break the law. On the contrary, we are to 'fulfil the law' by loving and serving one another (5:13, 14).

How is it possible to become holy? We have seen how Paul describes the Christian's inner conflict between 'the flesh' and 'the Spirit' and the way of victory through the ascendancy of the Spirit over the flesh. Those who belong to Christ, he says, 'have crucified the flesh', totally rejecting its evil 'passions and desires' (5:24). This is part of our repentance. It took place at our conversion, but we need to remember and renew it daily.

Christ's people also seek to be 'led by the Spirit' (5:18), to follow His 'line' (5:25) and sow in His 'field' (6:8), by disciplined habits of thinking and living, so that His 'fruit' will appear and ripen in our lives. This is the Christian way of holiness.

The last verse of the Epistle is a fitting conclusion: 'The grace of our Lord Jesus Christ be with your spirit' (6:18). For the Christian life is lived by the grace of Christ, and this grace (unmerited favour) is expressed in the three spheres which we have been considering.

First, the answer to the question of authority is *Jesus Christ through His apostles*. Christ appointed and authorized the Twelve and later Paul to teach in His name,[1] and promised them the Holy Spirit in special measure to bring His teaching to their remembrance and to lead them into all the truth.[2] So 'what Jesus began to do and teach' during His life (Acts 1:1) He continued through His apostles, and He intended men to submit to this apostolic authority as being His authority: 'He who receives you receives me', He said.[3] 'He who hears you hears me, and he who rejects you rejects me.'[4]

Secondly, the answer to the question of salvation is *Jesus Christ through His cross*. Jesus Christ came not only to speak but to save, not only to reveal but to redeem. On the cross He bore our sin and curse. And if we are in Christ crucified, united to Him by faith, all the blessings of the gospel—justification, adoption and the gift of the Spirit—become our personal possession.

Thirdly, the answer to the question of holiness is *Jesus Christ through His Spirit*. Christ not only died, rose and returned to heaven, but sent the Holy Spirit to replace Him. This Holy Spirit is the Spirit of Christ, who dwells in every believer.[5] And one of the greatest works of the Holy Spirit is to conform us to the image of Christ,[6] to form Christ in us (Gal. 4:19), to bring forth in our lives His 'fruit' of Christlikeness.

[1] Mk. 3:14; Lk. 6:13; Acts 1:15–26; 26:12–18 (especially verse 17 'I send you', *egō apostellō se*); 1 Cor. 15:8–11; Gal. 1:1, 15–17.

[2] Jn. 14:25, 26; 15:26, 27; 16:12–15.

[3] Mt. 10:40; *cf.* Jn. 13:20.

[4] Lk. 10:16.

[5] *E.g.* Rom. 8:9; 1 Cor. 6:19; Gal. 3:2, 14; 4:6.

[6] 2 Cor. 3:18.

So we have Christ through His apostles to teach us, Christ through His cross to save us and Christ through His Spirit to sanctify us. This in a nutshell is the message of the Epistle to the Galatians and indeed of Christianity itself. It is all included in the Epistle's last words: *The grace of our Lord Jesus Christ*—His grace through His apostles, His cross and His Spirit—*be with your spirit, brethren. Amen.*

The Message of Galatians

Study guide

STUDY GUIDE

It's all too easy just to skim through a book like this without letting its truth take root in our lives. The purpose of this study guide is to help you genuinely to grapple with the message of Galatians and think about how its teaching is relevant to you today.

Although designed primarily for Bible study groups to use over a six-week period, this series of studies is also suitable for private use. When used by a group with limited time, the leader should decide beforehand which questions to discuss during the meeting and which should be left for group members to work on by themselves during the following week.

To get the most out of the group meetings, each member of the group should read through the section of Galatians to be looked at in each study together with the relevant pages of this book. As you begin each session, pray that the Holy Spirit will bring this ancient letter to life and speak to you through it.

SESSION ONE

Galatians 1:1-24 (pages 11-37)

1 Read 1:1–5

a Paul describes himself as an 'apostle'. What does this mean (p. 13)? As we shall see, the very basis of Paul's message was being challenged by some in the Galatian churches. How does what he says here support his claim to authority (p. 14)?

b You might like to discuss together whether there are 'apostles' like Paul in today's church. What do you think he would have said?

c Ask one or more of your group to look up 'Galatia' in a Bible dictionary and a concordance and report back next time you meet. What can you discover about the background to this Epistle?

d Discuss together what you understand by the words 'grace' and 'peace' (1:3). Can you explain how they 'summarize Paul's gospel of salvation' (p. 16)?

e Some might see the crucifixion of Jesus as no more than the tragic end to a promising career. But Paul would not have agreed! What do we learn about the death of Christ from 1:4-5 (pp. 17ff.)?

2 Read 1:6-10

a In his other recorded letters to churches, Paul's opening greeting is followed by a note of praise and prayer. Why is this Epistle an exception (pp. 21ff.)?

b Paul attributes the problem to a group of troublemakers within the churches. What were they doing and why was it so damaging (p. 23)?

c How does Paul react and why is his response so strong (pp. 24ff.)? Can you think of similar situations in today's church? What can you learn from Paul's example?

d Paul insists here that 'there is only one gospel and that this gospel does not change' (p. 26). How then can we recognize the true gospel (pp. 27ff.)?

3 Read 1:11-24

a In the face of those who present a 'different gospel' (1:6), Paul now turns to defend the validity of his own ministry. What do his opponents say about him and the gospel he preaches? Where does Paul claim his message came from (pp. 29f.)?

b Try and trace through Paul's argument. What evidence does he give to support this astounding claim (pp. 30ff.)?

c The key question is whether or not Paul's gospel has a direct divine origin. In his own day, people claimed that he made it up or got it from someone else. What reasons do people give nowadays to question Paul's authority? How would you answer them (pp. 36f.)?

SESSION TWO

Galatians 2:1-21 (pages 39-67)

We saw in chapter 1 that Paul claimed to have received his message directly from God, not from men. But this raises a further question: was he preaching the *same* gospel as the church in Jerusalem? Paul answers this by describing two encounters with Peter and the other apostles.

1 Read 2:1-10

a Paul makes a further visit to Jerusalem, taking Barnabas and Titus with him. Why did some want Titus, a Gentile believer, to be circumcised? Why was Paul so insistent that this should not be done (pp. 42f.)?

b Why do you think Paul refers to the Jerusalem apostles in such a roundabout way in 2:6-9a? What was their reaction to the message Paul had been preaching (pp. 44f.)? What was it that led them to respond in this way?

2 Read 2:11-16

a Paul and Peter believed and preached the same gospel. But Peter was evidently not practising what he preached! What had he done which led to this public conflict with Paul? Why did he behave as he did? What was the result (pp. 50ff.)?

b Why did Paul react as he did (pp. 53ff.)? What was the long-term result (pp. 55f.)?

c What does he mean by the 'truth of the gospel' in 2:14 (pp. 54f.)?

d Can you think of anything in your life which effectively denies the truth of the gospel? What should you do about it?

e Can you think of any other situations where the truth of the gospel is compromised by the behaviour of those who claim to believe it? What does Paul's example prompt you to do about it?

3 Read 2:15-21

a What do you understand by the word 'justification' (p. 60)? Why is it 'central to Christianity' (p. 59)?

b Paul discusses the two possible routes to justification – 'by works of the law' or 'through faith in Jesus Christ' (2:16). What does he mean by 'works of the law'? In what way is this 'the fundamental principle of every religious and moral system in the world except New Testament Christianity' (p. 62)?

c Can you identify Paul's arguments in 2:16 and 21 which show that justification by works of the law, though a theoretical option, is actually impossible (pp. 63f., 66)?

d Paul anticipates a counter-argument in 2:17. What is it? How does he answer it (pp. 64f.)?

e Using this passage, how would you answer someone who said that justification by faith is merely a 'legal fiction' (p. 65)?

SESSION THREE

Galatians 3:1-29 (pages 69-102)

1 **Read 3:1, together with 1:6-10**

a What are the Galatians doing which leads Paul to call them 'foolish' (pp. 69ff.)?

b '... before whose eyes Jesus Christ was publicly portrayed as crucified' (3:1). How does this work out in practice today? To what extent do your Christian witness and evangelism do this (p. 74)?

2 **Read 3:2-5**

Paul shows the Galatians that they are wrong by reminding them first of their own past experience. Can you explain his argument (pp. 71f.)?

3 **Read 3:6-9**

Paul turns next to the Old Testament. The false teachers seem to have been saying that in order to become true sons of Abraham, Gentile converts had to keep the Jewish law and so, for example, undergo circumcision. How does Paul counter this (pp. 72ff.)?

4 **Read 3:10-14**

a Using Old Testament quotations to back up his

argument, Paul now expands on the two alternatives he discussed in 2:16. Why are those who 'rely on works of the law' (3:10) in trouble (pp. 78ff.)?

b Galatians 3:10 quotes Deuteronomy 27:26, the law's sentence of death for all who do not keep it. How then is it possible for anyone to escape the curse of 3:10 and 13 and enjoy the blessing of 3:14 (pp. 80ff.)?

c But this escape route is not automatic. Why not? What then do we have to do (p. 82)?

5 Read 3:15-18
How does Paul justify going right back to God's promises to Abraham and, on this issue, bypassing the law given to Moses (pp. 87ff.)?

6 Read 3:19-20
Verse 18 says that the law is not to be the means of our inheriting God's promise of blessing. What then *is* the law for (pp. 89f.)?

7 Read 3:21-22
a By making justification depend on keeping the law, the false teachers are setting God's law against God's promise and making them seem contradictory. How does Paul deal with this (pp. 90f.)?

b 'We must never bypass the law and come straight to the gospel. To do so is to contradict the plan of God in biblical history' (p. 93). How do your own Christian witness and evangelism stand in the light of this statement?

8 Read 3:23-29
a Paul continues by describing a similar pattern of law

and promise in individual Christian experience. What is the significance of the two images he uses to portray the law (pp. 96ff.)?

b But now those in Christ enjoy a new freedom. What specific blessings does Paul mention in these verses (pp. 98ff.)? Can you think of ways in which these work out in your own life?

SESSION FOUR

Galatians 4:1-31 (pages 103-129)

1 Read 4:1-7

a Paul now contrasts man under the law with man in Christ and draws out the implications for the individual Christian. How does he characterize man's condition under the law (pp. 104f.)? How does this work out in practice?

b In what sense did God send his Son 'at the right time' (pp. 105f.)? Why was he sent? In what ways was Jesus uniquely qualified to do the task set for him (p. 106)?

c Those in Christ have a new status through faith in him. But there is even more! What further blessing does the sending of the Spirit bring (pp. 106f.)?

2 Read 4:8-11

What was the basic mistake made by the Galatians (pp. 107f.)? What practical steps can we take to avoid falling into the same trap (pp. 109f.)?

3 Read 4:12-20

a Paul writes with great personal feeling, urging the Galatians to return to their former loyalty. What does he mean in 4:12 (pp. 111ff.)? How is this relevant for Christian ministers today?

b The Galatians once received Paul as they would have received Christ Jesus himself (4:14). Why had their attitude changed (pp. 113ff.)? What lessons does this have for us today (pp. 117f.)?

c What is the difference between Paul's attitude to the Galatians and that of the false teachers (pp. 115ff.)? What can we learn from this today (pp. 118f.)?

4 Read 4:21-31

a Paul turns to those who 'desire to be under the law' (4:21), and invites them to consider the logical outcome of their position. Why is physical descent from Abraham of itself irrelevant (pp. 122ff.)?

b Paul is saying that it's who your *mother* is that counts! In his allegory, what do Hagar and Sarah stand for (pp. 124ff.)? (See pp. 125-126 for an important note about 4:27.)

c 'Now we, brethren, like Isaac, are children of promise' (4:28). What two implications for the Christian community does Paul draw from this (pp. 126ff.)?

d 'The greatest enemies of the evangelical faith today are not unbelievers, who when they hear the gospel often embrace it, but the church, the establishment, the hierarchy' (p. 127). In what ways has this been true in your experience? Discuss what action you should take.

STUDY GUIDE

SESSION FIVE

Galatians 5:1-25 (pages 131-154)

1 Read 5:1–6

a Paul's argument is clear: if Christ has set us free from the law, how can we go back to living as its slaves? The specific issue is circumcision, something required by the false teachers as a necessary supplement to faith. What are the results c˜falling in with this demand? Why is this the case (pp. 132ff.)?

b Using this passage, how would you answer someone who said that Paul's emphasis on faith in Christ means that we can live as we please (p. 134)?

2 Read 5:7-12

a What marks of false teaching does Paul outline in this passage (pp. 135f.)? Why is it so difficult to keep preaching the truth (p. 137)?

b Paul's attitude to the false teachers (5:12) sounds harsh. What motivated him to feel this way about them (pp. 136f.)? What is your reaction to false teaching in the church today? What can you learn from Paul's example?

3 Read 5:13-15

a What does Paul mean by 'opportunity for the flesh' (5:13)? In what ways are you prone to misuse your Christian freedom in this way? What does Paul suggest as a possible antidote (pp. 140ff.)?

b Someone might argue that 'because Christ has set us free from the law, we can now ignore it altogether'. From 5:14, how would you answer this (pp. 142f.)?

4 Read 5:16-25

a Maintaining Christian freedom involves us in constant conflict between the 'flesh' and the 'Spirit'. What does Paul mean by these two words (p. 146)?

b A Christian friend of yours gets drunk one night, happens to read 5:21 the following morning and concludes that he has lost his salvation. How would you help him (pp. 147f.)?

c Christian victory in the conflict between the flesh and the Spirit comes as we crucify the one (5:24) and walk by the other (5:25). Discuss together what these two phrases mean in practice (pp. 149ff.).

SESSION SIX

Galatians 5:26 – 6:18 (pages 155-183)
Review (pages 185-191)

1 Read 5:26 – 6:5

a Paul deals now with some of the practical implications of 5:16-25. What is it that leads Christians to treat each other wrongly (pp. 156f.)?

b 'We have a divine burden-bearer who is quite adequate and ... it is a sign of weakness to require any human help' (p. 157). How would you answer someone who said this in response to 6:2 (pp. 157f.)?

c How do you explain the apparent contradiction between the instruction to 'bear one another's burdens' (6:2) and 'each man will have to bear his own load' (6:5) (pp. 159f.)?

d Galatians 6:1 is an example of a burden being borne. What guidelines does Paul give (pp. 160ff.)? How can you apply these today?

2 Read 6:6-10

a Paul's final few instructions are linked by the common theme that we reap what we sow. Discuss the ways in which 6:6 is relevant for you (pp. 167ff.).

b 'Holiness is a *harvest*; whether we reap it or not depends almost entirely on what and where we sow' (p. 169). What does it mean to 'sow to the flesh'? In what ways can we 'sow to the Spirit'?

c Are there areas in which you find yourself growing 'weary in well-doing' (6:9)? What does Paul say to encourage us (pp. 171f.)?

3 Read 6:11-18

a Paul opposes those who concentrate on outward show at the expense of what really matters, *i.e.* 'a new creation' (6:15). Can you think of modern examples of this conflict (pp. 176f.)?

b A further key issue concerns 'whether the essence of the Christian religion is human or divine' (p. 178). What does Paul see as the motive (pp. 179f.)? How is this relevant for you?

4 Review

Looking back over your studies in this Epistle, what major lessons stick in your mind? How do they compare with the author's summary (pp. 185ff.)?